Royal Arch Masonry
in Pennsylvania

Also from Westphalia Press

westphaliapress.org

The Idea of the Digital University

Masonic Tombstones and Masonic Secrets

Treasures of London

The History of Photography

L'Enfant and the Freemasons

Baronial Bedrooms

Making Trouble for Muslims

Material History and Ritual Objects

Paddle Your Own Canoe

Opportunity and Horatio Alger

Careers in the Face of Challenge

Bookplates of the Kings

Collecting American Presidential Autographs

Freemasonry in Old Buffalo

Original Cables from the Pearl Harbor Attack

Social Satire and the Modern Novel

The Essence of Harvard

The Genius of Freemasonry

A Definitive Commentary on Bookplates

James Martineau and Rebuilding Theology

No Bird Lacks Feathers

Earthworms, Horses, and Living Things

The Man Who Killed President Garfield

Anti-Masonry and the Murder of Morgan

Understanding Art

Homeopathy

Ancient Masonic Mysteries

Collecting Old Books

Masonic Secret Signs and Passwords

The Thomas Starr King Dispute

Earl Warren's Masonic Lodge

Lariats and Lassos

Mr. Garfield of Ohio

The Wisdom of Thomas Starr King

The French Foreign Legion

War in Syria

Naturism Comes to the United States

New Sources on Women and Freemasonry

Designing, Adapting, Strategizing in Online Education

Policy Diagnosis

Meeting Minutes of Naval Lodge No. 4 F.A.A.M

Royal Arch Masonry in Pennsylvania

William H. Paterson's

History of The Grand Holy Royal Arch Chapter of Pennsylvania and Masonic Jurisdictions Thereunto Belonging

WESTPHALIA PRESS
An imprint of the Policy Studies Organization

Royal Arch Masonry in Pennsylvania
William H. Paterson's *History of The Grand Holy Royal*
Arch Chapter of Pennsylvania and Masonic Jurisdictions
Thereunto Belonging

Westphalia Press
An imprint of Policy Studies Organization
dgutierrezs@ipsonet.org

For information:
Westphalia Press
1527 New Hampshire Ave., N.W.
Washington, D.C. 20036

ISBN-13: 978-1935907220
ISBN-10: 1935907220

Updated material and comments on this edition can be
found at the Westphalia Press website: westphaliapress.org

Editorial Note

The Royal Arch degree and the degrees associated with it are very old, but their relationship to the basic first three degrees of Freemasonry is still disputed. In 18th century America, Royal Arch rituals were worked in some lodges along with the initial initiatory degrees. The following pages give an excellent and concise description of the evolution of the Royal Arch in a state where it has always been influential.

As to origins, there is an argument that the famous Masonic third degree included Royal Arch work and that because this made the ceremonies too long, the Royal Arch was spun off. In England, the Royal Arch is included in the responsibilities of the United Grand Lodge, and the officers of the United Grand Lodge are also the officers of the Royal Arch.

This then is only an introduction to a complex situation, but a useful one. It goes behind the scenes to show how the present Royal Arch chapters emerged.

History of
The Grand Holy Royal Arch Chapter of Pennsylvania and Masonic Jurisdiction Thereunto Belonging
1795—1945

150TH ANNIVERSARY OF THE FORMATION

OF THIS GRAND BODY

An Address Delivered Before
The Grand Holy Royal Arch Chapter of Pennsylvania and
Masonic Jurisdiction Thereunto Belonging Convened to
Commemorate the One Hundred and Fifty Years

BY

WILLIAM J. PATERSON, *Past High Priest*
Temple Royal Arch Chapter No. 248

MASONIC TEMPLE
Philadelphia, Pennsylvania
December 6, 1945

Prepared at the request of Companion ROBERT J. ARNETT, *Most Excellent Grand High Priest, who at the Quarterly Communication of the Grand Holy Royal Arch Chapter of Pennsylvania, held at Philadelphia, Pennsylvania, on June 3rd, 1943, appointed Companion William J. Paterson, Past High Priest of Temple Royal Arch Chapter No. 248, Philadelphia, to write the History of The Grand Holy Royal Arch Chapter of Pennsylvania and Masonic Jurisdiction Thereunto Belonging, to be read at the One Hundred and Fiftieth Anniversary on December 6, 1945.*

By Way of Introduction

Upon this occasion we celebrate the Anniversary of One Hundred and Fifty years of "The Grand Holy Royal Arch Chapter of Pennsylvania and Masonic Jurisdiction Thereunto Belonging," together with the "Birth of Royal Arch Masonry in Pennsylvania," as early as the year 1758.

To have kept the light of Capitular Masonry burning upon the altar for so long a time is a heritage of which we, the members of this Grand Chapter are justly proud, and we trust that it may under "God's Will" spread its rays for generations to come.

The duty assigned to write the history of One Hundred and Fifty years of such a Grand Chapter, as the Grand Holy Royal Arch Chapter of Pennsylvania, has been taken seriously by the writer, and with a thought of sincere responsibility. But how shall human ability give appropriateness to words on this occasion? The riches of grateful feelings which fill the heart, are greater than the riches of language, and cannot always be expressed in words.

He realizes too, the task imposed upon him of rendering an account of this Grand Chapter's outstanding achievements during this long span of life, and it is his privilege now to bring before this Grand Body a sketch of the rise and procedure of Royal Arch Masonry as known in this Jurisdiction, as well as the formation and continuation of the Most Excellent Grand Royal Arch Chapter of Pennsylvania, to which is added in brief detail the exploration, and later the settlement of the site of Philadelphia by William Penn, the Birthplace of Capitular Masonry in America.

It has been the purpose to present only such matters as are deemed to be of sufficient importance for the reader, and in doing so it was necessary to delve through the minute-books, lengthy proceedings, miscellaneous papers and every known available source in order to find out what should be written; for to be aware of the origin and aims of an organization like this Grand Chapter, involves much labor and keen search for the truth, which is an elusive thing, and for this we have been seeking. The information gathered herein should arouse a deeper interest in the welfare of our fraternity. If the history has proven worth while, then the purpose has been accomplished and your historian has been amply repaid for burning the midnight oil.

The Grand Chapter has always been a forerunner for good in the ancient city of Philadelphia, and throughout the State, and we are proud of its past. Today its records afford convincing proof of its continued vitality. We trust its future history will reveal yet greater and nobler events.

The written accounts relative to the One Hundredth and the One Hundred and Twenty-fifth Anniversary celebrations of this Grand Body, and the histories of the local Chapters are rich in accomplishments relating to Capitular Masonry, and unfold the untiring labors of those Companions to whom this Grand Chapter is doubly indebted for its previous history of outstanding events. The list of happenings which appear in the records tell the true story in their own vocabulary. To publish here full details of all the occurrences during the past One Hundred and Fifty years would be utterly impossible. Again, there may be presented more than should be, but to include too much rather than too little is sometimes quite necessary to overspread the subject completely. By reason of the fact that this Grand Jurisdiction is not confined to its own border lines in regard to interchange of opinions from Grand Officers of other Grand Jurisdictions, we find correspondence with each other has resulted in a considerable amount of enlightenment, and will endeavor to cement our relations with each other for perpetuity.

4

We are thankful to the Supreme Architect of the Universe for his constant protection and goodness to all of us in these trying dark days and nights. We must continue on and do that which is good, anticipating that which is written in the Holy Scriptures and heard so frequently in the lecture of the Mark Degree, "and to receive at his hands a White Stone and in that Stone a new name written which no man knoweth saving him that receiveth it."

Adhering to the Ahiman Rezon, the Book of the Law of the Grand Lodge of Pennsylvania, and the Constitution of the Grand Holy Royal Arch Chapter of Pennsylvania, this history was submitted to Brother Scott S. Leiby, Grand Master of the Right Worshipful Grand Lodge of Free and Accepted Masons of Pennsylvania for his examination as to the symbolical material pertaining to the Grand Lodge of Pennsylvania, and to Companion William R. Burchfield, Most Excellent Grand High Priest of the Grand Holy Royal Arch Chapter of Pennsylvania for similar examination as to Capitular Masonry relating to the Grand Holy Royal Arch Chapter of Pennsylvania. Both of these Grand Officers have very affably given their approval of this historical narrative as effects Ancient Craft Masonry and Capitular Masonry respectively.

At this particular opportunity, I want to extend my appreciation to Companion John C. F. Kitselman, Most Excellent Grand Secretary, who has given me valuable assistance in preparing this history due to his faithful service of over twenty-five years in the Grand Chapter office; to Companion Robert J. Arnett, M. E. Past Grand High Priest for the privilege to serve Grand Chapter in the writing of this history, and to Companion George Hay Kain, Past High Priest of Howell Chapter No. 199, of York, Pennsylvania, for his kindness in permitting the use of portions of his "History of the Grand Holy Royal Arch Chapter of Pennsylvania," which he prepared in 1942 for the use of the General Grand Chapter in its proposed History of Royal Arch Masonry in the United States of America, which volume has not yet been published.

PRIMITIVE PHILADELPHIA

First to occupy this hallowed ground which later was to be called Philadelphia, was the Lenni-Lenape Indian Tribes. They seemed to have traveled from the West to the East and built their shelters or wigwams as they were then called, along rivers and small streams, all alone in the wilderness of this new country.

Henry Hudson, an Englishman, through historical research, was said to be the first European who on August 28, 1609, sighted the Bay now known as the Delaware.

In July 1610, we note over the same course another voyage was made by Captain Samuel Argall, who sailed up the Bay, and it was he who called it "Delaware" in honor of Thomas West, Lord De La Warr, Governor of Virginia.

In 1614, the United Netherland Company sent out Captain Cornelious Jacobson Mey, and a little later an associate of Mey by the name of Captain Cornelious Hendrickson sailed from abroad on a vessel sponsored by the Dutch East India Company, and reports show they discovered a large Bay and three Rivers.

In the early parts of the year 1623, one again finds Captain Mey sailing the high seas, being sent out by the Dutch India Company to command really the first ship to be sent direct to the American shores. It was on this trip the site of Philadelphia and the Delaware Bay were explored, and along the course until this day we find many landmarks of this early Dutch Exploration.

The Dutch were the first to venture here to explore and colonize this part of the country along both sides of the Delaware River and Bay. While they were very anxious to possess and govern these western shores, it was not favored by the Swedes and the English, who landed here for the very same purpose. However, the territory afterwards known as Pennsylvania was foreordained to be a Dutch Colony.

The settlement of the Swedes was another factor, for in 1638, a company financed by both the Dutch and Swedes founded the first Colony in America on the present site of Wilmington, Delaware. The triumph of the Dutch and the Swedes and whatever seemed to be their projects and dreams of hope were shattered and were of a short duration, for they had great difficulties in maintaining their early settlements which were doomed to be destroyed by the conquest of the British Power, as they finally lost what possessions they held in this part of the new world; for as early as the year 1634, two Englishmen settled as far up the Delaware as the present site of Philadelphia, and claimed both sides of the river which had originally belonged to the Dutch and the Swedes.

After years of various claims by the several explorers who had ventured thousands of miles for the sole purpose of discovering new settlements, there came the Treaty of Breda in 1667, whereby England was granted possession of the territory now known as Pennsylvania. Many of the Dutch and Swedish emigrants remained and built their homes in the new world.

William Penn

William Penn, a Quaker, received his education under strong Puritan influence, and devoted much of his time to religion. He was quite a young man and his ambition was to leave England and come to America with a thought of securing a plot of ground large enough to build a town whereby his people might enjoy freedom from persecution, and to be able to worship God in a manner most pleasing to them as Christians. Penn having studied maps and charts for many years enabled him to become well acquainted with the character of this country, and the British Government being indebted to his father, Admiral Penn, financially and in many other ways, the young Quaker was able to obtain a grant for a large tract of land upon which to build a colony.

The founding of Pennsylvania was confirmed to William Penn under the Great Seal of King Charles II, in 1681. Being now in possession of his Province, Penn immediately proceeded to persuade the good people around him to set sail, and settle in America where they would be free from constant fear.

The first colony, the brave pioneer to this new Province, left England in August 1681, in three ships. These emigrants were simply coming to America, because Philadelphia was not known at that early period.

William Penn directed Captain Holme, who had been commissioned by him as Survey-General of Pennsylvania, to set sail on April 23, 1682, and he arrived on the site of Philadelphia two months later. He started at once to lay out a principal City to be later the Capital of the Province, which Penn had in mind should be called Philadelphia.

On August 31, 1682, we find Penn leaving Deal, England, on the ship "Welcome," landing at New Castle, Delaware, on October 28, 1682, which is the accurate date of settlement and founding by Penn. However, on the same day we note his arrival in Pennsylvania at Upland, now Chester, and learn he did not take up his residence in Philadelphia until March 10, 1683, at which time it is said the first Seal of Philadelphia was adopted.

Penn, knowing the real meaning of the words "Brotherly Love" and being well informed regarding the Holy Scriptures, named the City, "Philadelphia." He did not judge the finances of anyone, considering first if the person was truly honest and willing to aid even those less fortunate. The question of nationality or creed mattered not with him, he made all welcome.

The spirit of Brotherly Love won for him the inspiring support of his people in the building of his town. It was Penn's desire that his Province should be a Christian town, of course to follow the Quaker customs, and he made it known from the beginning that the only condition necessary to hold citizenship or office was pure Christianity. Penn stated that Love and Obedience to God must prevail among his brethren, which we also find has been the teachings of Capitular Masonry from its inception.

The city having been made in accordance to his plans, we find him sailing for England in the year 1684. After an absence of fifteen long years he again set himself to embark for his Province, arriving in the month of October, 1699. He stayed for a period of two years, returning to England never to come back again. One of the last public acts of Penn in his Province was to present the City with the "Charter of Privileges" on October, 1701. In this Charter, Liberty of Conscience was assured to all who shall confess and acknowledge "One Almighty God" and live quietly under the Civil Government; and also that all who believe in "Jesus Christ" should be capable to serve the Government. By this act he constituted the town of Philadelphia as a City.

Although the city received this Charter from Penn's hands at this particular date, it appears to have had in effect the name and appearance of a city ten years previous, for we find the first Charter dated March 20, 1691. At this time Humphrey Murray was named and constituted by Penn as the first Mayor of the city, signing to its official acts. The original of this Charter is today preserved in the archives of the Historical Society of Pennsylvania. It is interesting to learn that his Grandson, Humphrey Murray, was the second Grand Master of the Grand Lodge of Pennsylvania in 1733.

Philadelphia continued in force until the end of the Proprietary System, when the Revolutionary War broke out, during which time the City was the seat of the Continental Congress except during the period of the British occupation. It was the

National Capital from 1793 until 1800, and was also the Capital of Pennsylvania continuously up to the beginning of the nineteenth century.

Penn's Green Country Towne (Philadelphia), growing from tall pine trees in the wilderness, is now an historical, educational and industrial centre, and its patriotism and loyalty to the nation has at all times been strongly manifested. It is said to be known as the most native American of all the large Cities in the United States, and Pennsylvania is the only State in existence which retains the name of its founder. Philadelphia is now known as the "City of Homes" and the "Workshop of the World."

FREEMASONRY IN AMERICA DURING THE EARLY EIGHTEENTH CENTURY

The Right Worshipful Grand Lodge of Pennsylvania being so finely dove-tailed in the structure of Grand Chapter, and the Grand Lodge having so willingly allowed the Grand Chapter of Pennsylvania to establish itself under the supreme supervision of Grand Lodge, and later to give its full consent to organize an Independent Grand Chapter of Pennsylvania in the year 1824, I believe a resume of "Early Freemasonry in Pennsylvania" and of "The Right Worshipful Grand Lodge of Free and Accepted Masons of Pennsylvania" should be here mentioned, knowing it would be most interesting to the Companions.

In the American Colonies, the story of the Beginning of Freemasonry, owing to the lack of documentary evidence, is shrouded in uncertainty. Masonic historians from all parts of the globe have continually made this subject a controversial one. Considerable interest has been shown concerning the facts pertaining to the first establishment of Freemasonry in the Western World, and additional data is here supplied from unexpected sources.

The Right Worshipful Grand Lodge of Pennsylvania has always felt that any history founded upon doubtful information is no better than a legend, and has conscientiously endeavored to support every material statement relating to its own affairs with incontrovertible proof.

11

It is fair to assume that in the year 1682, after William Penn had plotted his "Green Country Towne," some rugged pioneers who were Freemasons abroad, landed in Philadelphia, among whom were men of ability and distinction and who were given immediate posts of honor by England's Privy Council for the general supervision of the American Colonies.

If one will refer to the History of Philadelphia by Scharf and Westcott, he will find the earliest authenticated record of Freemasonry in a letter written in 1715 by one John Moore, who came to Philadelphia in 1703, as the King's Collector of the Port, in which he states that "he spent a few evenings in festivity with his Masonic Brethren in this City." Thus proving that brethren of the Craft dwelt in the Pennsylvania Colony at that particular early period.

We find in the early eighteenth century after the Grand Lodge of England was established in 1717, many Freemasons and their families from England and other parts abroad came to the shores on this side of the water and settled in certain sections of this country; what is known now as New Jersey, New York, Maryland, Virginia, the Carolinas, the New England States and Pennsylvania, which at that particular period were all British settlements. After being properly located here, naturally their interest in Freemasonry was renewed and Lodges were set up in their new land of adoption. We know without a doubt that records were made and kept in secret, but unfortunately some of the early minute-books have been lost or destroyed by fire.

On June 5th, 1730, His Grace, Thomas Duke of Norfolk, Grand Master of the Free and Accepted Masons of England, granted a Deputation to Brother Daniel Coxe, Esq., as Provincial Grand Master of the Provinces of New Jersey, New York and Pennsylvania, which was never revoked, modified or surrendered. He was given full power to nominate and appoint his Deputy Grand Master and Grand Wardens for the space of two years from the feast of St. John the Baptist next ensuing.

12

Further proof of this claim that Lodges were set up in this Province is gleaned from the fact that in Benjamin Franklin's Pennsylvania Gazette No. 108, for December 3rd to December 8th, 1730, it reads:—

> *"As there are several Lodges of Free-Masons erected in this Province, and People have lately been much amus'd with Conjectures Concerning them; we think the following Account of Free-Masonry from London, will not be unacceptable to our readers."* ***

We do know, however, through Masonic research that a St. John's Lodge was in existence and located in Philadelphia, sometimes mentioned as a Grand Lodge and as a Subordinate Lodge; and in Franklin's Journal began July 4th, 1730, he records his business dealings with "a Lodge of Masons" at Brother Hubbard's. There has also been found a Treasurer's Book of this Lodge known as "Liber B," commencing June 23rd, 1731, a set of By-Laws of St. John's Lodge June 5th, 1732, and successive notices of the meetings of Grand Lodge in Franklin's Pennsylvania Gazette. Franklin, however, fails to give any information as to when any of these Lodges were established.

The published records of the Craft in Franklin's newspapers supplant the early minutes, long since lost or destroyed. His connection with St. John's Lodge gives us an insight into the financial affairs of early Freemasonry as found upon the yellowing pages of "Liber B." Franklin's Masonic career extends over a period of sixty years, during which time he was accorded the highest Masonic honors at home and abroad. In the year 1734, Benjamin Franklin became Provincial Grand Master of the Provincial Grand Lodge of Pennsylvania, and during that year he reprinted Anderson's Constitutions of 1723, the first Masonic book published in America.

When the brethren who had been regularly made Masons in England, Ireland and Scotland or elsewhere abroad, came to

13

this Province they merely did what they had already done in their homelands, simply grouped their legitimate brethren together and formed a Lodge in Philadelphia, and at a later period a Grand Lodge adopting Rules and Regulations similar to those laid down by the Grand Lodge of England. These brethren owing to custom evidently desired a leader, and it was then that Brother Daniel Coxe, Esq., was appointed the first Provincial Grand Master for Pennsylvania by the then Grand Master of England.

Philadelphia in 1731, less than fifty years after the first coming of William Penn in 1683 to this Province, was the seat of the Grand Lodge of Free and Accepted Masons of Pennsylvania, and the Mother Grand Lodge of Freemasonry in the Western Hemisphere.

As early as June 24, 1731, William Allen, Esq., is mentioned as Grand Master of an Independent Grand Lodge in Philadelphia. In the Account Book of "St. John's Lodge of Philadelphia," the original ledger known as "Liber B" (now in possession of the Pennsylvania Historical Society) is an account with all the members of this Lodge from June 24th, 1731 to June 24th, 1738. The Lodge met on the first Monday of each month, and was constituted with thirteen members sometime prior to 1731, and without question was formed by "Immemorial Right," the same as the Grand Lodge of England was formed by the cohesion of Subordinate Lodges similarly formed by this method, not otherwise.

Following St. John's Lodge, which was the first Masonic Lodge working in Pennsylvania, we note Lodge No. 2 and Tun Tavern Lodge No. 3, (Moderns), working in Philadelphia, having been constituted the early part of 1749. A minute book of Lodge No. 3 is still in existence and the entries, however, show that this date was not the beginning of the Lodge, nor the earliest record of its minutes, and it is not positive that Tun Tavern was the original meeting place of the Lodge.

On June 24th, 1757, William Allen, Provincial Grand Master, warranted a new Lodge known as Lodge No. 4, and it was opened as a Modern Lodge. It started out with twenty members, several of whom were Royal Arch Masons (Ancients). Evidently these brethren did not know there was a "Modern" and an "Ancient" Grand Lodge of England. A controversy soon arose between the members of the three older "Modern" Lodges and the new Lodge. Brother George Brooks was the Worshipful Master of Lodge No. 4, and was also an "Arch Mason," a member of Lodge No. 183 in Belfast, Ireland. The officers of this new Lodge were finally summoned before the Grand Lodge, which thus resulted in detaining their warrant. Brother Brooks, the officers and members of Lodge No. 4, then petitioned the Grand Lodge of London for an "Ancient" warrant on January 10th, 1758. The Lodge continued on for about one year without a warrant. On June 7th, 1758, the warrant was granted as requested for a Lodge No. 1, in Philadelphia, and No. 69 in England, with Brooks as its Worshipful Master, thereby severing all connections with the three "Modern" Lodges.

After a time the "Moderns" became less active, many of them joining "Ancient" Lodges; others left the Province for political reasons, generally they were loyalists.

In the year 1760, the Lodge petitioned the Grand Lodge of England "Ancients" to warrant a Provincial Grand Lodge in Pennsylvania, assumed the No. 2, leaving No. 1, for the new Provincial Grand Lodge. William Ball, formerly a Modern Mason and having been made an Ancient Mason, was named on February 13th, 1760, as the first Provincial Grand Master, he having been balloted upon by the members and elected. On April 8th, 1760, the Lodge divided itself into two sections, the second section to be under the control of William Ball as Deputy Master.

The warrant for the Provincial Grand Lodge was granted July 15th, 1761, by Worshipful and Honorable Thomas Erskine,

Earl of Kelly, Grand Master of England. Due to this warrant being lost at sea, when a second warrant was issued and again we find this warrant was lost. Finally a third warrant was issued under date of June 20th, 1764, designating the Provincial Grand Lodge as No. 1 in Pennsylvania, and No. 89 in England, and confirming the date of the original warrant as July 15, 1761. The original warrant of 1758 had evidently disappeared, but as confirmed by the new Provincial Grand Lodge on February 10th, 1780, it imposed power as follows:—

> *"to admit, enter and make Masons according to the Ancient and Honorable Custom of Royal Craft, in All Ages and Nations throughout the known world."*

The warrant of the Provincial Grand Lodge authorized the Provincial Grand Master and his officers:—

> *"to grant dispensations, warrants, or constitutions for the forming, holding and well governing Lodges, within his Worship's jurisdiction aforesaid; and in his (or such other Lodge or Lodges by him authorized) to make and admit Freemasons according to the most ancient and honorable custom of the Royal Craft in all ages and nations throughout the known world."*

The Grand Officers of the new Provincial Grand Lodge agreed with the Lodge to divide Lodge No. 2 into two sections, the second section to be known as Lodge No. 3, and the warrant they received empowered the Lodge:—

> *"to make and admit Free Masons according to the most ancient and honorable custom of the Royal Craft, in all ages and nations throughout the known world."*

Therefore, this authorization given in the warrant proves very clearly the claim of power of the "Ancient" Lodges to confer the Royal Arch by the use of their Lodge warrants, following the original foreign custom of the Irish and Scotch Lodges.

When the General Grand Chapter was organized, the Grand Officers of that Body did not approve of the policy adopted in the eighteenth century to confer the first three degrees, Chapter degrees and even the higher degrees by use of a Lodge warrant, and claimed it was irregular to confer any Masonic degree by use of a Lodge warrant other than the first three degrees in Freemasonry.

It was evidently due to this decision that in the year 1824 led to the Independence of the Grand Chapter of Pennsylvania which had been under Grand Lodge authority in 1795.

On February 2nd, 1764, the new Provincial Grand Lodge of Pennsylvania was organized and the first movement on the part of the Provincial Grand Master after he was installed, was to constitute the second section of Lodge No. 2, into a separate Lodge to be known as No. 3. The warrant, however, was not actually issued until October 20th, 1767. By that time Lodge No. 3 was known as "Royal Arch Lodge No. 3." The first movement towards the separation of the members working the Royal Arch from the Lodge appears to have been on February 13th, 1783, when the brethren of that degree resolved upon a special night of meeting. A Seal for the Body was adopted in 1783, and the first By-Laws were adopted September 5th, 1789. These By-Laws established as a prerequisite for the Royal Arch Degree that the candidate should have been a Master Mason at least three years, and that he should have presided as Master of some regularly warranted Lodge six months, or that he shall have Passed the Chair by dispensation. They now speak of the Body as a Chapter and give it the name "Jerusalem," which Body remains today as Jerusalem Royal Arch Chapter No. 3, as well as Lodge No. 3, Free and Accepted Masons.

Therefore, through the "Moderns" Lodge No. 4, and its successor No. 1, and later No. 2, "Ancients," with its two sections, we trace Royal Arch Masonry, with Brother George Brooks and his Royal Arch associates, to a time "anterior to the year 1758."

BIRTH OF CAPITULAR MASONRY
IN PENNSYLVANIA

The precise date and circumstances of the origin of the first Royal Arch Lodge No. 3, coming to light in the year 1758, is somewhat hidden in obscurity. However, this Body has continued on from that date up to the present time, and as stated above, is known as Jerusalem Royal Arch Chapter No. 3, the title "Jerusalem" given to the Chapter in 1789.

In order that we may have some meager vision of the period of 1758, just one hundred and eighty-seven years ago, let us delve into the past for a brief survey. The population of the entire United States was a few less than a million five hundred thousand souls. Pennsylvania, together with Delaware, had a population of less than two hundred thousand people. Philadelphia, at that time, was much larger than New York City, but contained only about fifteen thousand inhabitants. Yet her excellent buildings, cleanliness, and care for education signalized her over every other city. It was not until the year 1686 that the printing press had been introduced and a public high school in 1689. The present University of Pennsylvania was previously established in 1740 as a Charitable School, and became the University of the State of Pennsylvania in 1779, and later in September 1791, received its Charter.

In 1758, however, one of the greatest men in English history, Sir William Pitt, was called to the head of the British Government, and everything felt his influence.

THE OLDEST KNOWN AMERICAN ROYAL ARCH SUMMONS.
USED BY LODGE No. 3, A. Y. M., PENNSYLVANIA.

Engraved by Henry Dawings, Philadelphia, **Circa 1765.**
Original 9 x 6½ in. in Archives of Grand Lodge.

On May 28th, 1758, Amherst, with twenty-two ships, fifteen frigates, and an army of ten thousand men, after a long passage, reached Halifax, and started up the Nova Scotia coast. On June 8th, 1758, they embarked at Louisburg, and began a siege which lasted until July 27th, 1758.

On July 8th, 1758, Abercrombie was defeated by the French at Fort Ticonderoga, and on August 27th, 1758, Bradstreet took Fort Frontenac.

On Saturday, November 25th, 1758, Fort Duquesne was captured by the British, and renamed Fort Pitt, now Pittsburgh, in honor of Sir William Pitt, to whom America has raised many statues to his name.

This was the year in which Pennsylvania, animated by an unusual military spirit, raised twenty-seven hundred men for the expedition of conquest of the Ohio Valley, which was subsequently led by Brother George Washington. Among these recruits were Benjamin West, the celebrated painter, and Anthony Wayne, then a boy of thirteen. Such were some of the stirring events of this particular year.

This century, which also gave birth to Franklin, Washington, Wellington and Napoleon, and a host of other brilliant characters, gave birth to Royal Arch Masonry in Pennsylvania, which means to us one of its greatest events. Men of noble ideas and brave deeds pass to the beyond, but other memories live on only in the minds of those who really knew them. Yet the principles of Royal Arch Masonry will continue to live as long as time itself shall continue to exist.

It was Laurence Dermott, the energetic and zealous secretary of the Ancients, enthusiastic of the Royal Arch, who in 1756, said, "The Royal Arch, I firmly believe to be the root, heart and marrow of Masonry."

History comes to us, either orally when it may be termed tradition, or else by writing and printing, and it is well for those who do not know, that the minutes of Royal Arch Lodge No. 3, "Ancients" from December 3rd, 1767, are still in existence and being carefully preserved in the Library of the Grand Lodge of Pennsylvania.

At a previous meeting prior to the above date, a Brother John Hoodless was proposed by three members of the Lodge, "All Royal Arch Masons." On December 9th, 1767, the Lodge decided not to admit him as he belonged to the Army, and "was of the opinion it would not be proper to enter, pass and raise any person in the Lodge belonging to the Army," as there is a lawfully warranted Body of Good and Able Masons in the Royal Irish Regiment, and also a promise had been made to that Body by our Deputy Grand Master and ourselves."

In 1768, the minutes of the Lodge show various payments "in the preparation for the Royal Arch," "fixing the Vails," "treasurer's jewel," and "two triangles," "iron for the Arch," etc. The Lodge also had in its possession a pedestal, floorcloth, crowns and scepters, proving the Lodge was very active at that period and degrees were continuing to be conferred.

Harmony Royal Arch Chapter No. 52

This Chapter was the next Royal Arch Body and was organized April 28th, 1794. It was through the efforts of five Royal Arch Masons, who secured the use of the warrant of Harmony Lodge No. 52, that a Royal Arch Chapter was formed, taking the name and number of the Lodge, conferred the Royal Arch on four brethren on this date, and later in the same year added six more names to their membership and eleven additional names in 1795. This Chapter unfortunately entered into an irregular proceeding which caused much dissension, which was quickly healed, and through this action resulted in the formation of the Grand Chapter of Pennsylvania.

The Grand Chapter of Pennsylvania—1795

Thirteen Lodges being represented, a letter was received and read, signed by Brother Matthias Sadler as Grand High Priest of a Grand Royal Arch Chapter, by him "said to be established under the several warrants of Lodges Nos. 19, 52 and 67, held in the City of Philadelphia."

A petition was signed by two members of Lodge No. 52, one of whom was Grand Secretary, and was presented and read, "stating some irregular proceedings on the part of the Master and some members thereof." At the same time some of the members of Grand Lodge issued a complaint against the three Lodges mentioned, when the warrants were called in and suspended until the next Grand Communication. A committee was appointed to inquire into the facts set forth in the petition from the two members of Lodge No. 52, and into other matters relative to the disturbance.

On November 23rd, 1795, the committee reported to Grand Lodge, when the officers and members of the Lodges whose warrants were suspended, were permitted to be present during the reading and discussion of the report, and the late Worshipful Masters of the three Lodges, another Brother of Lodge No. 19, seven other brethren of Lodge No. 52, and a Brother of Lodge No. 67 were admitted. Matters of importance were talked over numerous times as the report of the committee was a lengthy one.

The full report of the Committee containing the following facts respecting a pretended new Chapter of Royal Arch Masons attempted to be instituted in this city reads thus:—

"1. That it is declared and avowed by the members of the pretended new chapter that they differ from the ancient mode of working in this city, insomuch that they cannot agreeably to their principles admit to visit their said Chapter any of the old-established Arch Masons—and they have in fact refused so to do in divers instances—and that those not in union with them may be conducted through a considerable part of their work, unsubjected to any restraint."

"2. That the innovations were introduced by an individual, by the name of James Molan, who is admitted and acknowledged to have been the only person in this city who pretended to know the degree as given in the said new Chapter, and who has not been able to furnish credentials of his having ever been regularly made a Mason in any degree, and on different occasions has given contradictory accounts."

"3. That the Chapter held under the authority of No. 52 was improperly and arbitrarily declared to be dissolved, as well by the presiding officer thereof as by the Worshipful Master of No. 52—the new scheme introduced in lieu thereof, without authority of that Lodge, and the written protestations of certain members thereof notwithstanding."

"4. That the said James Molan, not a member of any Lodge under this jurisdiction, having himself, without assistance, made two persons by the names of Brown and Denys, those three opened what they call a Chapter under the pretended sanction of No. 19's warrant, used for that purpose without the authority of that Lodge being first obtained."

"5. That the said Molan and his associates, in the absence of the Worshipful Master of Lodge No. 67 and without his consent or knowledge, or the officers or members, availed themselves of the sanction of the warrant of his Lodge, to introduce this mode of working."

"6. That several brethren having been thus pretendedly arched by Molan and his associates, and getting these three warrants under this Grand Lodge into their possession, and having arched two brethren, one from Maryland and the other from Georgia, and con-

sidering those as having the force of three Lodges, under the jurisdiction of Pennsylvania, and of one under that of Georgia, and one under that of Maryland, they resolved themselves into a pretended Grand Royal Arch Chapter of Pennsylvania."

"7. That now having, as they suppose, erected under the sanction of five regular constituted Lodges, their Grand Chapter, they pretend not only to work without the sanction of any warrant, but arrogate a power to grant from themselves warrants to others, and do not acknowledge themselves to be under the jurisdiction of this Grand Lodge."

"8. That sundry members of the Lodges under the jurisdiction of Pennsylvania, who were Companions of the established Chapters, have attached themselves to Molan and acknowledged his assumed powers and pretended Chapter."

"9. That the Master of No. 67, Brother Baum, has given full and ample testimony to your Committee that his error has only arisen from want of caution and misapprehension of the advice and opinion of some old brethren, and that so far as his name and concurrence appear connected with these irregular proceedings, it has been in a great measure without his knowledge and approbation; and further, that on finding the imposition and evil tendency of the measures, he withdrew himself and has given the most ready obedience to every order and requisition, and an unequivocal evidence of his resolution to persevere in discountenancing any such proceedings."

"Whereupon your Committee propose the following resolutions:—

"Resolved, 1. That the said James Molan ought not to be considered and received as a Mason by the

23

Lodges or brethren under your jurisdiction, and that his conduct in assuming a character and powers not belonging to him has had a tendency to mislead many worthy brethren, to introduce an unhappy schism amongst the Lodges and ought to be discountenanced."

"Resolved, 2. That neither of the three Lodges under your jurisdiction has authorized the pretended workings of Molan or his followers in the Royal Arch degree, and that the presence of two brethren from other States unknown to us and assisting in these practices without the concurrence of their Lodges, even if they were respectively Masters of Lodges under other jurisdictions, could not give validity to their proceedings, and was irregular and disorderly, and tending to destroy the harmony of the brethren in this State and that which has hitherto so happily existed between the Lodges and brethren of the several States."

"Resolved, 3. That therefore the said pretended Grand Royal Arch Chapter cannot be considered as legal, and that the brethren should be ordered to withdraw from and discountenance the same, and that in the meantime no brother who has joined in their proceedings shall be admitted into any Lodge under this jurisdiction until he shall have made such satisfaction as shall be deemed sufficient by the Right Worshipful Grand Lodge."

"Resolved, 4. That the suspension of the three warrants, so far as respects the faithful brethren, be withdrawn, and that the R. W. Grand Master be requested and authorized to do whatever may be necessary and proper for enabling such brethren of those Lodges to carry on the work of their Lodges, and if necessary, to elect and constitute new officers.

"*Resolved, 5. That Brother Baum, Worshipful Master of Lodge No. 67, ought not to be considered as subject to any censure of this Grand Lodge, but shall be in full and good standing.*"

"*Resolved, 6. That your Committee have designedly not entered into a discussion respecting the names of the individual brethren who have been culpable on this occasion, from a wish to avoid unnecessary severity, and yet, as it is to be feared some have erred from a disposition inimical to the good order and harmony of the craft, the Committee recommend that the Lodges be ordered to report to a Committee, to be appointed by the Grand Lodge, the names of all such as have been concerned therein, that further inquiry may be had into their respective conduct.*"

"*Your Committee propose also the following resolutions:—*

"*Whereas, The supreme Masonic jurisdiction over all Lodges of Ancient York Masons, held in Pennsylvania, has uniformly been and is duly and legally vested in the Grand Lodge of Pennsylvania;*

"*And whereas, The officers of the different Lodges under the jurisdiction of the said Grand Lodge are constitutionally members of the Grand Lodge, although they may not have obtained any degree above that of Master Mason;*

"*And whereas, It is the acknowledged right of all regular warranted Lodges, so far as they have ability and numbers, to make Masons in the higher degrees, and as it is possible that some differences may exist or innovations may be attempted to be introduced in*

25

those higher degrees, which for want of some proper place of appeal may create schism among brethren;

"And whereas, Since many years there has been established in this city, according to ancient forms, a Royal Arch Chapter, under the sanction of the warrant of Lodge No. 3, whose work has met with the approbation of all visiting Royal Arch Masons from the different parts of the world;

"And whereas, The number of Royal Arch Masons is greatly increased, insomuch that other Chapters are established in this city and in other parts of Pennsylvania;

"And whereas, It was always contemplated that such Chapters, regularly held, should be under the protection of this Grand Lodge;

"And whereas, It is the prevailing wish of the Royal Arch Masons within this jurisdiction that a Royal Arch Grand Chapter should be opened under the authority of this Grand Lodge;

"Be it therefore, and it is hereby resolved, That a GRAND ROYAL ARCH CHAPTER be opened, under the immediate sanction of the Grand Lodge of Pennsylvania;

"Be it further resolved, That all past and existing officers of the Grand Lodge having duly obtained the degree of Royal Arch, and all past and existing officers of Chapters of Royal Arch Masons, duly and regularly convened under the sanction of a warrant from the Grand Lodge of Pennsylvania, be considered as members of the Grand Royal Arch Chapter, and that all members of regular Chapters shall be admitted to their meetings, but not have any vote nor speak to any question, unless requested.

"Be it further resolved, That the said Grand Royal Arch Chapter shall hold one stated annual meeting on the day preceding St. John the Evangelist in each year, and occasional Chapters when necessity requires, and shall have powers to elect all its officers, saving that of R. W. Grand Master of the Grand Lodge for the time being, if of that degree, shall always preside as High Priest; that the said Grand Royal Arch Chapter make its own By-Laws, and shall hear and decide upon all complaints and appeals from Chapters held under warrants, to be issued under the authority of the Grand Lodge. But the said Grand Royal Arch Chapter shall not at any time raise any brother to the degree of Royal Arch."

The report and the resolutions therein contained were unanimously adopted and agreed to; it was ordered that Brother Matthais Sadler be furnished with a copy of the report and resolutions; a Committee was appointed to carry into effect the sixth resolution; and two hundred copies of the proceedings were ordered to be printed and transmitted to all the Lodges in this jurisdiction, and to such Grand Lodges in Europe and the different States in America and elsewhere with whom the Grand Lodge corresponds.

On November 30th, 1795, the Committee reported that it had met on November 27th with several brethren of the new Chapter and that:—

"The following resolutions of a Committee from the lately established Chapter were agreed to by their conferees on behalf of the whole Chapter, viz:

"Resolved, That we consent and agree to dissolve the Grand Royal Arch Chapter formed under the warrants of Lodges Nos. 19, 52, and 67.

"Resolved, That as Masons, we acknowledge the supreme jurisdiction over all Lodges in Pennsylvania

*to be vested in the Grand Lodge of Pennsylvania, and
that without the sanction of a warrant from or the
authority of the said Grand Lodge, no Lodge or
Chapter can be legally opened or held within the
jurisdiction of the said Grand Lodge."*

*"The Committee of the Grand Lodge in conse-
quence of the above resolutions, do recommend the
following resolution, expressly leaving the said Chapter in the situation it now is if this resolution is not
adopted;*

*"Resolved, That there now exists a perfect harmony
among the brethren in Pennsylvania, and that the several brethren who have been suspended be and are
hereby restored, and that all matters and things done
in the Grand Lodge, affecting the private and individual rights of the said brethren, be and are hereby
done away and repealed."*

The resolutions were thereupon unanimously adopted; the
suspended warrants were restored; the suspended members
who had joined the late Grand Royal Arch Chapter were restored to their former situation and dignity; the Grand Master
congratulated the brethren upon the renewal of harmony;
"gave such advice as was suited to the occasion;" and the
Grand Secretary was directed "to make the minutes of this
communication as publicly known as those of the preceding
meetings."

A Royal Arch Chapter was opened according to Ancient
Form on December 22nd, 1796 by a number of the brethren,
when resolutions of the Grand Lodge were read and adopted,
authorizing a Committee to be appointed to frame Rules and
Regulations for the Grand Chapter.

On December 26, 1796, an election was held, when certain
Rules and Regulations were adopted for the good of the Order.
Then followed the usual form of securing a seal, plate device,

and a form for certificates. The Grand Master presided over the meeting, at which time there were chosen a Grand King and a Grand Scribe.

In the year 1798 it is noted for the first time that the three ranking officers were designated as "Grand Chiefs," and the Grand Body was usually known as a "General Grand Chapter of the Holy Royal Arch." This Grand Body was only opened occasionally, owing to the lack of insufficient members in attendance. On May 30th, 1796, the Grand Lodge received several communications from the Grand Lodge of England which were read, containing Rules and Regulations for the government of their Holy Royal Arch Chapter as supported by the "Ancient" Grand Lodge of England, and approved of the "fairness and justice" which was "manifested upon the pretended assumption of a Grand Lodge or Chapter of Royal Arch Masons being formed independent of and without sanction of your R. W. Grand Lodge."

In similarity to the English rules, the Grand Chapter on February 24th, 1798, adopted fourteen Rules and Regulations for the government of the Grand Holy Royal Arch Chapter which were approved by Grand Lodge on March 5th, 1798. The preamble sets forth the Pennsylvania position as to the Royal Arch Degree in a manner very similar to that taken in 1813, in the Articles of Union of the United Grand Lodge of England. The preamble declares:—

> *"Ancient Masonry consists of four degrees: the three first of which are that of the Apprentice, the Fellow-Craft and the Sublime degree of Master: and a brother being well versed in these degrees, and having discharged the offices of his Lodge, particularly that of Master, and fulfilled the duties thereof with the approbation of the brethren of his Lodge, is eligible, on due trial and examination by the chiefs of the Chapter to whom he shall have applied and by*

them found worthy, of being admitted to the fourth degree, The Holy Royal Arch."

"It follows, of course, that every regular warranted Lodge possesses the power of forming and holding Lodges in each of those several degrees; the last of which, from its preeminence, is denominated amongst Masons a Chapter."***

"That no Chapter of Holy Royal Arch shall be held or convened within the Commonwealth of Pennsylvania or Masonic Jurisdiction Thereunto Belonging, but under the authority and sanction of a regular subsisting warrant granted by the Grand Lodge according to the old institutions, and by the consent of said Lodge first signified to the Grand Chapter."***

"That no brother shall be admitted into the Holy Royal Arch but he who has regularly and faithfully passed through the three progressive degrees, and has filled and performed the office of Worshipful Master in his Lodge to the satisfaction of his brethren, or passed the chair by a dispensation of the R. W. Grand Master upon the recommendation of his said Lodge,"

"That a General Grand Chapter of the Holy Royal Arch shall be held half-yearly on the third Monday in June and December in each year; that every warranted Lodge shall be directed to summon its Excellent Royal Arch Members to attend the same, and that none but past and present officers of Chapters duly and regularly formed under the sanction of a warrant from the Grand Lodge of Pennsylvania, and registered, and past and present Grand Officers (Being Royal Arch Masons) shall be members thereof; and Royal Arch Masons, members of private Chapters and certified sojourners, to be admitted as visitors only."***

30

Passing to the Chair

Originally the Royal Arch Degree was conferred only on actual Past Masters. Other brethren were anxious to receive the degree, and so, under the "Ancients" and in Pennsylvania, there arose the practice of "Passing to the Chair," and thus qualifying for the Royal Arch Degree, brethren who had never presided over a Lodge by election, but who were recommended for the honor by the Lodge or its officers. This ceremony— it is not a degree—is performed in the Lodge of which the applicant is a member, by virtue of a dispensation from the Grand Master (or a District Deputy Grand Master). This dispensation is granted only to Master Masons of six months' standing, on recommendation of the Lodge officers, payment of a fee to the Grand Lodge, and after the Lodge votes to act under the dispensation.

The practice began in Pennsylvania as early as February 5th, 1783, when:—

> *"the Grand Master, at the particular request of the attending brethren, dispensed with the forms, and passed Brother Joseph Howells, Jr., to the chair as the Master of a Lodge, and he was saluted by the brethren accordingly."*

The ceremony is similar to the actual installation of a Worshipful Master and is in effect the Degree of "Past Master," conferred as the second degree in the Capitular system of other jurisdictions.

In 1912, a proposition to include the Degree of Past Master among the Chapter degrees was reported adversely in Grand Chapter as being an infringement on the prerogatives of Grand Lodge. In 1926, Grand Lodge made no objection when Grand Chapter abolished "Passing to the Chair" as a capitular prerequisite.

The Vision Towards Independence

On September 7th, 1812, a number of brethren belonging to different Lodges in the city were in the habit of attending a Mark Lodge held in Apple Tree Alley, between Fourth and Fifth Streets, which Lodge professed to work under a warrant or dispensation issued by Ezra Ames, styling himself General Grand Scribe of the General Grand Royal Arch Chapter of the United States of America, dated at Albany, New York, December 19th, 1811. This Lodge professed to give the Mark in a different manner from the other Lodges in this city, and declared it to be a degree beyond that of Master Mason, and as preparatory to an exaltation to the Holy Royal Arch.

The Grand Lodge, having learned through a committee appointed by the Grand Master of this degree being conferred, disapproved "of any meeting of Masons in this city under warrants from other jurisdictions, and have never acknowledged any such authority as the Grand Holy Royal Arch Chapter of the United States of America." They therefore recommend and enjoin the members of the subordinate Lodges under their jurisdiction to abstain from and avoid all such meetings. It appears that these letters of dispensation issued by the said Ezra Ames, were never ratified or confirmed by the General Grand Royal Arch Chapter of the United States of America, nor had they been extended by any of the officers of that Body. Nevertheless, on November 25th, 1816, Thomas Smith Webb, Deputy General Grand High Priest of the General Grand Royal Arch Chapter of the United States of America, did recall the letters of dispensation, by letters issued under his hand and seal, and directed to William G. Oliver, of the City of Philadelphia, issued as aforesaid, and required the said William G. Oliver, and his associates, "to abstain hereafter from all assembling together or conferring any degrees of Masonry under the authority derived from the said Ezra Ames."

The committee further reported that they "find themselves obligated to express their regret that there should have been, in the first instance, any interference with the Masonic Jurisdiction of the Grand Lodge of Pennsylvania, yet they state with pleasure that every reparation that could be offered by the said General Grand Chapter or its officers, has been made, and that they have evinced a desire to remain on terms of Brotherly Love and Friendship with this Grand Lodge, and to abstain from collision on points on which these Bodies are known to disagree."

It appears that from about 1812 that members of Chapters seemed more interested in Freemasonry than usual, for we note under date of January 4th, 1813, a new set of Laws, Rules and Regulations were read, debated by paragraph, and unanimously adopted by Grand Chapter and subsequently by Grand Lodge. However, with a few minor changes the new Laws provided that Grand Chapter should meet Quarterly instead of Semi-Annually, on the third Monday in February, May, August and November of each year. The Grand Tyler shall be allowed one dollar and fifty cents each meeting for tyling, serving notices, etc., to be paid out of the funds of the Grand Chapter.

A great deal of confusion seemed to arise at various intervals. The Grand Chapter on March 17th, 1813, had requested Grand Lodge to authorize it to require every Chapter to submit to Grand Chapter its By-Laws, Rules and Regulations and to grant to Grand Chapter the power of deciding exclusively upon them. Grand Lodge declined to grant such request. A committee was appointed on May 15th, 1815, in Grand Chapter to create new laws or suggest such alterations whereby the Grand Chapter could more thoroughly exercise its rights.

On November 8th, 1821, Chapter No. 51 made known its desires and requested Grand Chapter to take into consideration the propriety of adopting some rule or order for the interest of its members so that they may participate in the general benefits of Arch Masonry throughout the United States. However, the committee appointed and the wishes of Chapter No. 51 were discharged without report on May 20th, 1822.

From this date on we find meetings were held and resolutions were proposed to change laws, causing confusion in the minds of the members, and the unrestful situation finally ended after a period of two more years when in 1824, the Grand Chapter of Pennsylvania was given its Independence.

It was on May 20th, 1822, when a set of resolutions for reorganization of the Grand Chapter was presented and referred to a Special Committee in conjunction with a Committee which had been appointed by Grand Lodge under a resolution intro- duced on January 7th, 1822:—

"to inquire into the expediency of changing the existing form of government of Royal Arch Masonry, and if found expedient to digest and report to this Grand Lodge such a system of government of Royal Arch Masonry as in their opinion, may be best calculated to advance the prosperity of Royal Arch Masonry, without impairing the supreme authority of the Grand Lodge over the same or diminishing the revenues of the Grand Lodge."

At the next meeting of Grand Lodge held April 1st, consid- eration was given to the resolution offered on January 7th, when on motion the said resolution was amended by striking out the last clause, which is as follows:—"Without impairing the supreme authority of the Grand Lodge over the same, or dimin- ishing the revenues of the Grand Lodge." The resolution was then laid upon the table.

On June 17th, the sundry resolutions proposed by the Grand Chapter of May 20th, for the organization of the Grand Chap- ter, were presented and read, when it was resolved, "that a Committee of five members of the Grand Chapter and five of the Grand Lodge be appointed to make a report to decide and make proper report." Whereupon, on motion and seconded, "the resolution laid on the table on the 7th of January last relative to the appointment of a committee to inquire into the expediency of Royal Arch Masonry, amended by the Grand Lodge on the first of April last, was taken up for consideration and adopted as amended." At a meeting of Grand Lodge held September 16th, 1822, when these two committees made their report, it was again laid on the table.

On August 19th, the Grand Chapter Committee did not approve of the adoption of the resolution and proposed a new set of substitute resolutions, a portion of which was as follows:—

"That nothing herein contained shall be considered as a recognition by the Grand Lodge of the degrees of Royal Master, Most Excellent Master, and Mark Master as degrees of Ancient York Masonry."

The Grand Chapter on November 18th, which had approved the report, voted to reconsider its action and on December 7th, 1822, referred the report to another committee:—

"To inquire what measures are necessary to be taken in order to preserve to the members of the subordinate Chapter under the jurisdiction of this Grand Chapter, their rights and privileges as Royal Arch Masons."

On December 30th, 1822, a proposed constitution for the governing of Grand Chapter was reported and duly considered on January 6th, 1823. However, a motion was made to postpone the further consideration, when a substitute resolution was offered, declaring that Ancient Masonry consisted of four degrees, that it was competent for all Lodges possessing a lawful warrant to open a Chapter and exalt Masons to the supreme degree of Holy Royal Arch, and that the existence of a Grand Holy Royal Arch Chapter is unnecessary where there exists a Grand Lodge, and that the Grand Chapter "be and is hereby adjourned sine die."

On February 26th, 1823, it was resolved, "that a committee of seven brethren be appointed to inquire if any, and what grievances, exist in Arch Masonry, and report a remedy for those grievances or errors to the Grand Committee for their consideration and adoption." It was reported by the committee on December 28th, 1823, "that grievances do exist in Arch Masonry."*** that previous to the year 1795, there was no Grand Chapter of Holy Royal Arch Masons held in the United States."*** In the same year "a Grand Royal Arch Chapter of Pennsylvania, was opened under the sanction of the Grand Lodge of Pennsylvania, which has continued its meetings until the present time," and that "the right to exalt to the degree of the Holy Royal Arch, under the warrant of a regular Lodge, never appears to have been questioned under the formation of the Grand Chapter (later the General Grand Chapter) in 1798," at which time a convocation from different States in the Union of Arch Masons was held at Hartford, in the State of Connecticut, and a Grand Chapter formed." Regulations were adopted at this convention, stating that no person can be recognized as an Arch Mason unless he has been exalted under the authority of some warrant granted by a Grand Chapter, "thus at one stroke cutting off all the Arch Masons on the face of the globe from all intercourse or communication with them."

Previous to that time and since, except where those regulations prevail, a warrant regularly granted by an acknowledged Grand Lodge has been considered a sufficient and the only proper authority to work in all the degrees of Ancient Masonry."***

As at present organized and conducted, your committee think the Grand Chapter of Pennsylvania stands too much isolated from the Grand Lodge, and that measures ought to be adopted to unite them more closely, and thereby give increased life and vigor to the drooping state of Arch Masonry. This committee stated for the purpose of remedying the foregoing evils, they offer additional regulations and ask that they may be incorporated with and become a part of the standing regulations of the Grand Lodge of Pennsylvania.*** It shall be the duty of the Grand Chapter, as soon as may be after the adoption of these regulations, to take measures to open a correspondence with the other Grand Royal Arch Chapters in the United States.*** The report of the Grand Committee was considered and adopted by the Grand Lodge, when on motion, it was ordered to be printed and copies furnished to each of the Lodges under the Jurisdiction of the Grand Lodge.

Meanwhile, Grand Chapter on June 23rd, 1823, approved the Constitution which the committee had reported to it on the preceding December 30th, and adopted the following resolution:—

> "That it be recommended to all the brethren who now are or hereafter may become Royal Arch Masons, to make themselves acquainted with the honorary degrees of Mark Master and Most Excellent Master, as the means of enabling them to meet and act with their brethren in Arch Masonry throughout the United States."

The Grand Lodge on November 3rd, approved the system which had been recommended by the Grand Chapter Committee on August 19th, 1822, which, after adoption Grand Chapter had voted to reconsider. However, there is one difference. The resolutions of Grand Chapter as they appear in the proceedings and are quoted above, provide that nothing shall be considered as a recognition of the degrees of Royal Master, Most Excellent Master, and Mark Master "as degrees of Ancient York Masonry." The Grand Lodge proceedings omit the degree of Royal Master from the group. This may have been by intention or a typographical error.

The resolutions were tentatively adopted and confirm the position of Pennsylvania that only the three Symbolic Degrees, with the Royal Arch, comprise Ancient Craft Masonry; although one will note that when the two Grand Bodies finally agreed in the formation of "The Independent Grand Chapter of Pennsylvania" this particular clause was omitted.

The Grand Lodge took action in which it declined to coincide in the proposed Constitution presented by Grand Chapter, after which the Grand Chapter on November 28th, 1823, voted to "non-concur" in the system approved by Grand Lodge, and appointed a Conference Committee, when a like committee was appointed by Grand Lodge. The committee on conference reported on December 24th, and the Grand Chapter adopted a proposed Constitution. This constitution January 5th, 1824, was reported to Grand Lodge, was amended, and as amended was adopted. The Grand Chapter on February 16th, 1824, adopted the Constitution as amended. This Constitution was to go into operation "in and from and after" the semi-annual meeting in May next.

INDEPENDENCE OF GRAND CHAPTER

The Constitution claimed complete independence of the Grand Chapter from the Grand Lodge with one exception, as quoted in Article III, "that the Grand Chapter shall annually pay over to the Grand Lodge the balance of money on hand after deducting their expenditures, to be appropriated to the Sinking Fund, until the debt now due to the Grand Lodge shall be paid, after which the Grand Lodge shall have no claim upon the funds of the Grand Chapter but the same shall be at their own disposal."

All through the prolonged conferences the new suggested system included only the Mark and Most Excellent Master Degrees as a part of the Chapter work. It seems it was not necessary for a Companion to be a Past Master in order to receive the Mark degree, but Passing to the Chair was a requirement before having conferred upon him the two higher degrees in Capitular Masonry. However, such is not the case at the present time.

The General Grand Chapter's constitution of 1806 did not permit separate Past Master's Lodges, or Most Excellent Master's Lodges. In Pennsylvania measures were taken to warrant separate Mark Lodges and Most Excellent Master Lodges.

On May 17th, 1824, the Grand Chapter was opened in "Ancient and Solemn Form," and forthwith closed in harmony, sine die." Immediately following this meeting, eleven companions met for the purpose of organizing themselves into a Grand

Holy Royal Arch Chapter under and by virtue of the Constitution approved of and adopted. They wanted to be relieved of the responsibility to the Grand Lodge, so far as its legislature and the details of regulations of its inner working was concerned. The able management of these Companions enabled the business of Grand Chapter to be carried on in the most creditable manner for a number of years. They started out by appointing temporary Grand Officers, the first three being mentioned as First, Second and Third Grand Chiefs, who were to hold office until an election be held for officers by virtue of the said Constitution, and they adjourned until May 24th, when they elected the following Grand Officers, as Grand High Priest, Grand King, Grand Scribe, Grand Secretary and a Grand Treasurer. The Grand Secretary's station prior to the above date seemed to have had various titles, such as Grand Scribe, Grand Registrar or Grand Recorder.

Rules and Regulations for the government of the Grand Chapter were adopted July 16th, 1824, and on October 8th, various forms of warrants for Chapters, Mark Lodges and Most Excellent Lodges were decided upon, and the first warrant was granted to George Washington Chapter No. 133, at Chambersburg, Pennsylvania. Warrants were granted to Chapters Nos. 3 and 51, on November 15th, 1824, and on December 20th, Harmony Chapter No. 52, was granted a warrant, and at this meeting it was on motion, resolved:—

> *"That the Grand High Priest proceed forthwith to install himself in the office of Grand High Priest of this M. E. Grand Holy Royal Arch Chapter for the ensuing twelve months from St. John's Day next, and that he then install the Grand King, Grand Scribe, Grand Secretary and Grand Treasurer in their respective offices for the like period, thereupon Companion Michael Nisbet was duly installed M. E. Grand High Priest and the other officers were duly installed in the several offices to which they had been elected."*

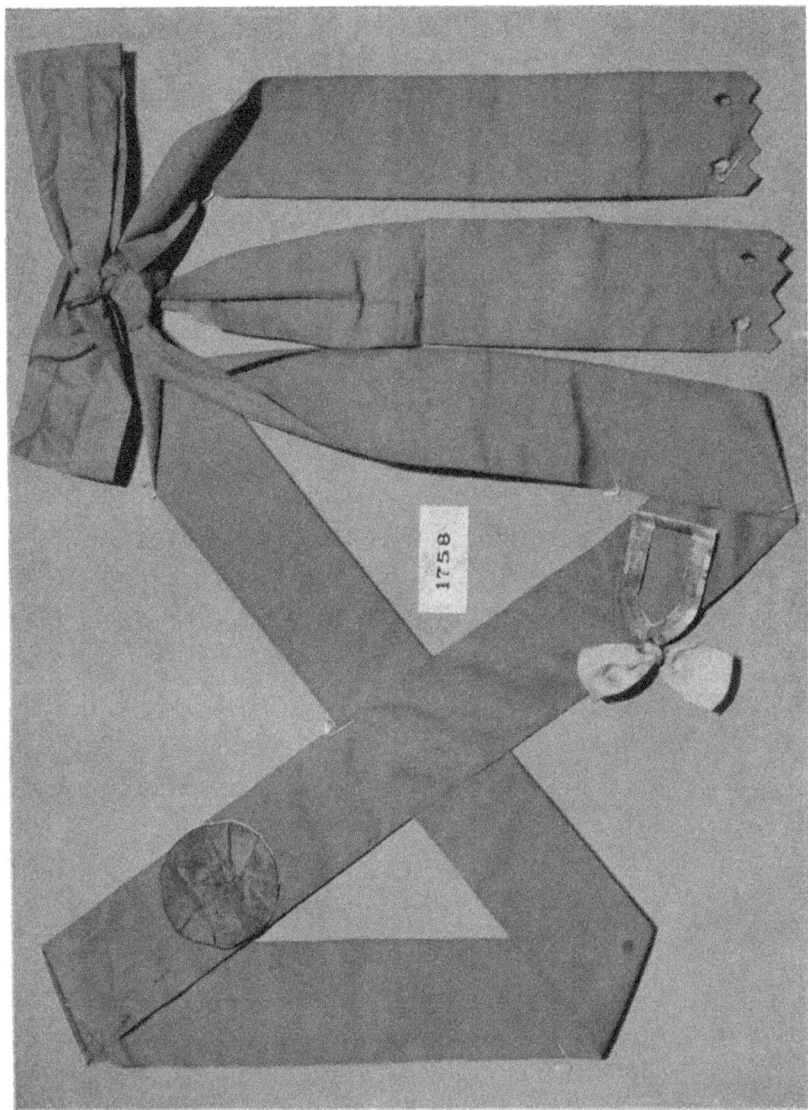

ROYAL ARCH REGALIA OF BRO. WILLIAM BALL.
FIRST GRAND CHIEF.
GRAND CHAPTER OF PENNSYLVANIA—1795.

Original in Museum of Grand Lodge.

At the Annual Grand Communication held December 27th, 1824, on motion, it was resolved:—

"That it is of the first importance that a full and distinct understanding should exist between the R. W. Grand Lodge of this State and this M. E. Grand Chapter in regard to suspensions and expulsions under their several jurisdictions."

A mutual understanding was had between the Right Worshipful Grand Lodge of Pennsylvania and the Grand Holy Royal Arch Chapter of Pennsylvania, and from this date up to the present day "Peace and Harmony" has prevailed.

However, there were certain Lodges that contended they retained the right to confer the succeeding degrees as theretofore, by virtue of their Lodge warrants.

The Grand Lodge on March 7th, 1825, adopted the following resolutions:—

"Resolved: that the Grand Lodge transmit to each of the subordinate Lodges under its jurisdiction a copy of the Constitution, Rules and Regulations for the government of Mark Master Masons' and Most Excellent Master Masons' Lodges, and of the Royal Arch Chapters within the bounds of its jurisdiction."

"Resolved: that the Grand Lodge do recommend to all the Lodges of Mark Master Masons and Most Excellent Master Masons, and to all Chapters of Royal Arch Masons within the bounds of its jurisdiction, to conform to the provisions contained in the said Constitution, Rules and Regulations."

"Resolved: that no Lodges under this jurisdiction has by the virtue of the warrant of the Grand Lodge, the right hereafter to confer any other degrees than those of the Entered Apprentice, Fellow-craft, Master Mason and Past Master, and that no brother can re-

ceive the degree of Past Master unless duly elected
Worshipful Master of a particular Lodge, or by virtue
of a dispensation regularly issued and obtained for
that special and specific purpose."

At the Adjourned Quarterly Communication of Grand Lodge
held April 18th, 1825, a resolution was presented to withdraw
Mark Lodges and the Mark Degree from the Grand Chapter,
which was not approved.

At the Adjourned Quarterly Communication of Grand Lodge
held June 19th, 1826, the committee appointed September 5th,
1825, to inquire whether any violations of compact between
the Grand Lodge and subordinate Lodges, with respect to the
dues and contributions assessed upon the latter, had taken
place, made report, stating, in substance, that the sums charged
by the Grand Chapter for Chapter warrants are, respectively, an
increase of the price for warrants beyond the sum paid at the
time of the compact above referred to, and that the Grand
Lodge had, through inadvertance (the constitution of the Grand
Chapter being adopted subsequently to, and not in the manner
set forth in the compact), violated the first proposition thereof.
After much discussion during the meeting of the Committees
appointed by Grand Lodge and Grand Chapter, the final resolution was adopted on September 4th, 1826, after it had been
approved by a majority of the Lodges.

"Resolved: that the constitution of the Grand Holy
Royal Arch Chapter, so far as it authorizes the Grand
Chapter to make rules and regulations for the gov-
ernment of Holy Royal Arch Masonry, and thereby
confers the power to receive fees for granting war-
rants to Holy Royal Arch Chapters under their jur-
isdiction, and for other services, be and the same is
hereby confirmed."

On December 4th, 1826, the resolution was adopted and a
few minor changes were made, such as "under their jurisdic-

tion" and word "Confirmed" were changed to read, "within their jurisdiction" and "approved and confirmed."

The Grand Holy Royal Arch Chapter of Pennsylvania by the adoption of this resolution finally established its permanent independence.

We must not forget that from 1822, during which year Companion Josiah Randall was Grand High Priest until 1824, agitation for a constitution giving to the Grand Chapter full control of its affairs, was incessant, aggressive and intelligent. The members of the Grand Chapter were also members of the Grand Lodge. Human nature, then as now, caused them to run to the extreme points of vituperation in their discussion, and failure and disaster were predicted and prophesied in case of consent of the Grand Lodge should be given, but constant hammering of such companions as Grand High Priests Michael Nisbet, Tristram B. Freeman, Thomas Kittera, and a number of others who were able men and leading citizens, the object for which they had contended was accomplished finally and completely in Grand Chapter, and in Grand Lodge, both Bodies agreeing to the Independence of Grand Chapter.

Anti-Masonic Movement

The business of Grand Chapter was conducted in an even and fraternal spirit for a time under the able management of the above named, until the Anti-Masonic Craze started in the year 1826, which cast a dark shadow over the Masonic horizon and swooped down upon our heads, and like a pestilence disabled our working force to such an extent that it required strong men to stand up for the faith that was in them. Petitions were circulated against Freemasonry, and introduced into the Legislature, the brethren were denounced from the rostrum as well as the pulpit, the envenomed darts of bigotry and intolerance being chiefly hurled at all the Lodges and Chapters.

The effect of this crusade soon became apparent among the members of all Masonic Bodies, the brethren gradually dropped off under the great pressure, social, religious and political, brought to bear upon, until there were a few of their members left. As the dark clouds of political excitement continued to gather during the Anti-Masonic period, 1826-1832, and the outlook for the brethren became darker and darker, the Anti-Masonic candidate eventually being elected Governor of the State, the Masonic bodies at last succumbed to the pressure brought to bear by the fanatics and their misguided followers, so that in the year 1835, the few remaining brethren who had the courage to avow themselves as Masons, had difficulty to exist.

However, the fanaticism that woeful enemy to reason finally spent its fury and resurged into oblivion after nearly twenty years of effort to destroy Freemasonry, leaving the Masonic Fraternity unscathed in the minds of all right thinking people, upheld as it was by the brethren who had stood firm in their belief in the days of trial and tribulation. Grand Chapter, respected abroad and at home, content with itself, with the prospect of a bright future which it has fully realized, continued to prosper and today stands out like a beacon light, a guidance to our companions in Capitular Masonry.

While this pestilence was checked to a certain extent and had caused much unrest in the fraternity, our companions were only waiting for the opportunity to again meet with their companions.

Revival of Capitular Masonry

In the year 1846, we find the Grand Chapter holding three communications, the first on May 18th, with three Chapters represented, four Past High Priests, three visitors and a total of twenty-seven companions present out of eight Royal Arch Chapters, and one Mark Lodge with a total membership of about two hundred and fifty.

The first announcement made, was the reopening and reorganization of Chapter No. 150, at Washington, Pennsylvania, on March 10th, 1846. The Grand Chapter was holding its communications promptly in the Masonic Hall (formerly known as Washington Hall) on Third Street above Spruce in Philadelphia. The meeting room was small and inadequate for conferring Capitular degrees, and Grand Chapter requested Grand Lodge on several occasions to make such alterations suitable for Royal Arch purposes. Grand Chapter was indebted to Grand Lodge for rent, with no prospects of immediate payment, and Grand Lodge itself was also in a very poor financial condition, and it was noted that no alterations-were made.

However, our companions were looking forward and continued to march straight ahead for we read that from 1846 to 1870, there were constituted sixty-six new Chapters, two Mark Lodges, and the membership had increased to 7,119. A revival had surely commenced, Grand Chapter was holding communications four and five times a year; the recall of old warrants, new applications for Mark Lodges and new Chapters were pressing this Grand Body, so it is very evident that the brethren wanted Capitular Masonry, and they were proud of it.

In 1847, Chapter No. 150, at Washington, agreed to celebrate the coming Saint John the Baptist's Day with a public procession, but the Grand Secretary notified this Chapter that the rules and regulations prohibited all public parades as Arch Masons, Grand Chapter, like human nature, itself, cannot move successfully on without something happening at times, and it is well that it does, for frequently it brings closer relationship and a better understanding with each one concerned.

At the Fourth Communication held November 15th, 1847, the Grand Secretary read the following correspondence, which was ordered to be filed, to wit:—Which was a letter sent to the Grand Secretary of the Grand Chapter of New York under date of June 18th, 1847, stating: "In 1843 or 1844, a companion attempted to visit a subordinate Chapter in New York and was refused admission on the ground that the Grand Chapter of Pennsylvania did not recognize the Grand Chapter of the

United States, and asked whether it is by the direction of the Grand Chapter of New York that subordinate Chapters refuse to admit a visiting companion from our Chapters."

On June 25th, 1847, the Grand Secretary of the Grand Chapter of Pennsylvania received a letter from the Grand Secretary of the Grand Chapter of New York wherein he said: "I have only to state that the subject has never been before the Grand Chapter of this State; consequently, no such direction has been given and he would lay the communication before Grand Chapter at its next meeting in February." However, there was no further correspondence on this subject.

At the Quarterly Communication held August 16th, 1852, owing to the intimate relations between the Grand Lodge and the Grand Chapter, and to prevent any misunderstanding in the future, a committee was appointed to examine the records of the Grand Lodge and the Grand Chapter in regard to the compact made between the Grand Lodge and the Grand Chapter at the separation of these two Bodies. The committee was directed to report, if possible, at the next meeting of the Grand Chapter.

At a Quarterly Communication held November 15th, the committee made a full and complete report of extracts from the minutes, and they summed up by saying:—

"The Grand Chapter will perceive from these extracts, embracing all that has taken place on the subject-matter of this report, from December 7th, 1812, to January 5th, 1824, when the present constitution was approved of by the Grand Lodge, that no compact, agreement or understanding, of any kind whatsoever, other than the Constitution itself, was entered into between the Grand Lodge and Grand Chapter. A disposition of this kind was certainly exhibited in a clause of the resolution offered in the Grand Lodge on the 7th of January, 1822; this clause, however,

was subsequently withdrawn by the Grand Lodge itself."

The report was received and adopted.

At the Annual Communication held December 27th, 1852, one can judge of the financial condition of the Grand Chapter, when the Grand Treasurer presented his report of receipts during the past six years as $1,767.82 and the payments during that period $1,276.62, leaving a balance on hand of $491.20.

On December 27th, 1853, we find the funds of Grand Chapter had dwindled to $371.24, and on motion the Grand Treasurer was directed to pay this balance to the Grand Lodge, agreeable to the provision in the Constitution of Grand Chapter.

At the Quarterly communication held February 20th, 1854, a note was attached to the minutes which read:—

"One hour after the regular hour. The lateness of the hour, and small attendance, was caused by a severe snow storm, the heaviest for the past forty years."

On February 19th, 1855, at a meeting of Grand Chapter the following resolution was adopted:—

"Resolved: That a committee of three be appointed to confer with a committee appointed by the Grand Lodge in relation to fitting up and furnishing the New Hall, on Chestnut Street."

On August 20th, 1855, a Quarterly communication was held, when printed proceedings were received from a number of Grand Chapters, which were referred to the Committee on Correspondence, their special attention being called to the action of the Grand Chapter of Illinois which had refused admittance to Royal Arch Masons from this State. The committee was directed to report as early as possible before the Dedication of the New Hall. At this meeting the sum of $500.00 was directed to be paid to the Grand Lodge.

New Masonic Hall — 1855

The Quarterly Communication held November 19th, 1855 was held in the New Masonic Hall on Chestnut Street, between Seventh and Eighth Streets, Philadelphia (North side).

At the Quarterly Communication held August 18th, 1856, a resolution was offered strictly prohibiting the Grand Treasurer from paying any more money to the Grand Lodge of Pennsylvania, which resolution was laid over.

At an Adjourned Quarterly Communication held October 6th, when the Committee on Foreign Correspondence made the first report noted in Grand Chapter, it was a report full and complete, worthy of the committee whose names were appended to the report. It was a "retort courteous" to the attack made upon the Grand Chapter of Pennsylvania and its Royal Arch Masons by the Grand Chapter of Illinois, and approved by the Grand Chapters of Ohio and New York.

Attempts had been made for some years to force this Grand Chapter to unite with the General Grand Chapter, and Illinois resolved to close the doors of their Chapters against Royal Arch Masons of Pennsylvania because we did not confer the Past Master's Degree in the Chapter, and because our Royal Arch Masons, "Passed the Chair" before taking the Mark Master's Degree. (The committee's report was a lengthy one and can be read in full in the proceedings of Grand Chapter, 1895, pp. 71-72.)

The Grand Chapter thought so much of this report as to order it specially printed together with extracts from a most able report by Companion Anthony O'Sullivan of the Grand Chapter of Missouri, on the same subject.

After the report had been read to Grand Chapter, the Grand Secretary was directed to forward a copy of the Rules and Regulations of this Grand Chapter to the Grand Chapter of Illinois with Article IV, of the Constitution and "Admission of Members" in the Rules and Regulations marked for its information.

At the Quarterly Communication November 17th, 1856, a companion from Chapter Kittanning desired to visit Grand Chapter, when the Grand High Priest declined to admit him. A resolution was offered to admit him, and in a vote of 32 ayes and 15 noes, he was admitted.

An Adjourned Quarterly Communication was held December 18th, 1856, when a resolution was adopted to pay no more money to the Grand Lodge. However, it will be noted under date of December 28th, 1857, the Grand Treasurer of the Grand Chapter was directed to pay to the Grand Treasurer of the Grand Lodge one thousand dollars. The Grand Secretary, then by permission of Grand Chapter, appointed a Deputy Grand Secretary.

The Quarterly Communication of Grand Chapter held November 16th, 1857, at which time the Grand Officers were elected for the first time, a companion residing outside the City of Philadelphia was elected Grand King. The Annual Communication was held on December 28th, when the Grand Officers were installed.

At the Quarterly Communication held on May 17th, 1858, Companion Joseph S. Riley offered the following for the consideration of the companions, viz:—

> *"Whereas, By the report of the committee on accounts, made this evening, it appears that the annual income of this Grand Chapter has continued to increase until, as shown in the report of the committee, to be over four times the amount of the annual disbursement, viz: the receipts being $1,334.23, while the payments were but $320.50."*

> *"And Whereas, The Grand Chapter has no provision made for Charitable purposes, whereby, relief may be afforded to worthy and deserving Companions, their widows or children, who may be in necessitous circumstances; therefore be it:—*

49

"Resolved, That one-half of the income of this Grand Chapter be appropriated and specifically set apart for the purpose of forming a 'Charity Fund' for the relief of worthy Companions, their widows and children who may be in circumstances as justly to need our assistance."

"Resolved, also, that the Grand High Priest and the Grand Treasurer, for the time being, be charged with the duty of annually investing the same, also any income growing out of said investment, until the same shall amount to the capital sum of five thousand dollars."

"Resolved, that the above provisions go into effect this year. When the above 'Fund' shall have attained the sum of five thousand dollars, it shall be the duty of this Grand Chapter to make provision for its just and equitable disposition."

At the Quarterly Communication held February 21st, 1859, the resolution of May 17th, 1858, in relation to a Grand Chapter Charity Fund, was called up, when the following was adopted:—

"Resolved, That the sum of one thousand dollars of the funds now in the hands of the Grand Treasurer be appropriated as the foundation of a Grand Chapter Charity Fund, and that the same be invested by the Grand High Priest and Grand Treasurer for that purpose."

"Resolved, That the subject be referred to the Committee on the Constitution, to devise and report a plan for the establishment, regulation and government of a Grand Chapter Charity Fund."

The Most Excellent Grand High Priest at the Quarterly Communication held May 16th, 1859, informed Grand Chapter that in conformity to the instructions of the Grand Chapter, and in conjunction with the Grand Treasurer, he had invested $1,000.00 in City 6% Loan, as the foundation of a Grand Chapter Charity Fund.

At the Annual Grand Communication held December 27th, 1860, the Most Excellent Grand High Priest spoke of the outbreak of the Civil War, with words full of patriotism, appealing to Masonry, to use its influence in the then condition of affairs, and said:—"But Masonry is not a piety, but patriotism"—

> *"Its teachings, its spirit and its influence tend to the highest welfare of the State or country in which Masons reside. A bad citizen can never be a good Mason. He who violates the laws of the land will not be particular as to his adherence to the Landmarks or rules of our Order, which among other things, enjoin upon us 'to be peaceful citizens,' and cheerfully to conform to the laws of the country in which we reside, not to be concerned in plots and conspiracies against our government, but patiently to submit to the decisions of the Supreme Legislature. We are members of a great Brotherhood. Whatever, therefore, comes home to us, or befalls our country, having a direct connection with the peace and safety of ourselves and families, or the welfare and happiness of our brethren, commands our attention and interest as Masons and citizens.****

> *"That this union, the work of our fathers cemented at the first with their blood and consecrated by a thousand hallowed associations is about to rent asunder. ***That States which heretofore revolved in harmony around a common centre are about to rush against each other, as to make foes of those who have been pledged as brothers."****

"American Masonry was born of pure and noble parentage, and rocked in the cradle of our country's revolutionary struggle.***The roll of her members contains the names of many of the greatest men and purest patriots that this or any other country has ever produced.*** The Arch of our Masonic Union like a bow of promise, now spans this continent. Under its ample canopy are not less than 5,000 Lodges and Chapters and over 300,000 Masons—all men of greater or less influence, and all having received the same conservative and patriotic teaching. In our Masonic Union and Brotherhood there are no sectional parties or divisions to heal; no balance of power between North and South to maintain; no Mason and Dixon Line to divide. All are members of the same fold; if true Masons they are the most powerful conservative element now in this nation whether residing in Pennsylvania or South Carolina, they must regard each other as Brethren, and not for one moment do or countenance any act that looks to arraying brother against brother."

"Let us then arouse to our duty, call to mind and practice our Masonic teachings in relation to our country and each other; exert the influence we possess as citizens, as truly and effectually as did our fathers in the 'days that tried men's souls' speaking with a voice that shall be heard, the sentiments of Washington and Jackson, 'this Union must not—shall not be severed, unless by consent and agreement'."

At the Quarterly Communication held August 20th, 1866, an invitation was received from the Grand Lodge of Maryland to participate in the Laying of the Corner-Stone of the New Masonic Temple, in Baltimore, on November 20th, which was declined, as it was not in accordance with the customs and usages of Royal Arch Masonry in this Jurisdiction for Royal Arch Masons to take part as such in any public ceremonies or processions.

The Chairman of the Committee on Correspondence under date of December 27th, 1867, at the Annual Grand Communication of Grand Chapter presented a report wherein he stated, that "since the return of peace has enabled us to receive the fraternal greetings of many Grand Chapters which were shut out from communication with us by the iron cordon of war, we now welcome them to our tabernacles and our hearts with that warm Masonic sympathy which during four weary years of strife and blood we never ceased to feel."**** Whereupon a resolution was offered and adopted:—

"Resolved:—That the Grand Chapter of Pennsylvania will unite with all Royal Arch Masons in other jurisdictions in cementing the bonds of Masonic Union and Charity between the Grand Chapters and Companions, and of friendship between the people of the two sections of our country, which were recently at war with each other."

The Most Excellent Grand High Priest then spoke, saying:—

"What influence Masonry had in assuaging the horrors of war is evinced by the various Masonic Soldiers' Relief Associations, and the thousands of Masons meeting in their Lodges, or on the field of battle, or in the wards of the military hospitals. Those who left their homes for the front of battle were freed from annual dues by their Lodges and Chapters, and their homes and little ones looked after, and when necessary, cared for by their brethren in Masonry. We do not claim that Masonry did more than others, but we do assert that the work of Masonic Charity was done as all Masonic work should be done in secrecy.

Masonic Charity should be known to but three: the giver, the receiver and the Mason's God."

At the Quarterly Communication held February 3rd, 1870, an amendment to the constitution was adopted, when $1,500.-00 was ordered to be invested in the New Masonic Temple Loan, and $2,000.00 was appropriated for expense of the Grand High Priest for the year 1870.

At the Quarterly Communication May 5th, two hundred dollars was appropriated to the relief of destitute surviving sufferers of the late calamity at the State Capital at Richmond, Virginia, and $2,500.00 was ordered to be invested in the New Masonic Temple Loan.

At the Quarterly Communication held on November 3rd, the system of Grand Representative was begun by acknowledging of a Grand Representative from the Grand Chapter of Louisiana and also from Oregon, near the Grand Chapter of Pennsylvania, and so satisfactory were these appointments that they have been continued uninterruptedly until the present day. It was also at this time the beginning of procuring portraits of Past Grand High Priests, Grand Treasurers, and Grand Secretaries was started. This has resulted in the complete collection of portraits which now adorn the walls of the Grand High Priest's room, and today we enjoy the fruits of this wise measure.

Twenty-five years ago seventy-five Chapters, with a membership of seven thousand, constituted the Grand Chapter of Pennsylvania, now we have enrolled one hundred and twenty-one Chapters with a membership of over sixteen thousand, truly wonderful growth, indicating unparalleled prosperity. Foreign Grand Chapters were commencing to ask for recognition and we note on November 3rd, 1871, the Grand Chapter recognizing the Grand Mark Lodge of England and Wales.

At the Quarterly Communication of Grand Chapter held February 1st, 1872, the Special Committee on Charity Fund made a report suggesting certain amendments to the Constitution, action on which was postponed until the next Quarterly Communication which was held on May 2nd, when the proposed amendments were taken up, considered, amended, and adopted, as follows:—

Regulations for the Committee on Charity

1st: *"The Committee on Charity shall receive and hold in trust all moneys and securities bequeathed, granted, or appropriated for a 'Grand Chapter Charity Fund'; make all investments on account thereof; such investments to be made under the style and title of 'The Trustees of the Charity Fund of The Grand Holy Royal Arch Chapter of Pennsylvania'; report their proceedings and the state of the fund annually to the Grand Chapter, or whenever required by the Most Excellent Grand High Priest, and conform to such rules and regulations as may be enacted by the Grand Chapter for the government of such fund. No investments shall be made on account of the fund except in bonds and mortgages and ground rents (when the same are a first encumbrance on real estate), the stocks or loans of the Grand Lodge of Pennsylvania, the United States, the State of Pennsylvania or the City of Philadelphia; and the Trustees shall have no power to alter or change any investment without the sanction of the Grand Chapter, given at a regular Grand Communication thereof, or at a Special Grand Communication called for that purpose. The income derived from the fund shall not be appropriated in any way (except for reinvestment) until the principal thereof amounts to the sum of twenty-five thousand dollars."*

2nd: *"When the principal of the Grand Chapter Charity Fund shall amount to the sum of twenty-five thousand dollars as aforesaid, then the Grand Chapter shall provide rules and regulations for the distribution of the interest (or such proportion as may be thought proper) for the relief of Companions or Mark Master Masons in distress."*

The Most Excellent Grand High Priest said at the Annual Communication on December 27th, 1872:—

"What has been done during the past was done with the best of intentions, and for the advancement of the Grand Chapter. As we look forward to the future, we anticipate with peculiar pleasure the occupancy of a New Temple, in which the architect and builders have combined all that wisdom, strength and beauty could suggest. How many of us may live to tread its halls, we know not. Before its dedication many may have the vail of blindness of this world lifted from their eyes and they will behold the Master Builder in his Eternal Temple.

"In leaving this old Temple and taking up our abode in the new, may we leave behind us all the bitter animosities, hatred and bickering of life, and enter upon the discharge of our duties before God and Man with a firm determination to live up to our instructions as Royal Arch Masons. May you and I feel the satisfaction of a peaceful heart and conscience this day twelve months, with nothing to regret during that time."

As the time for dedicating the New Masonic Temple was drawing near and the governing bodies of Blue and Royal Arch Masonry have so long worked together in harmony, it was deemed proper that the Grand Chapter should assist in giving expression to the joy of the fraternity on the completion of the New Masonic Temple. The Grand Officers were appointed a committee to contract for and have built, in the

Renaissance or Grand Chapter Hall, an organ for the use of the Grand and subordinate Chapters. The organ was erected in a manner novel in the construction of that Grand instrument, the pipes and mechanism being supported over the head and the rear of the organist.

At the Quarterly Communication held May 1st, 1873, the Grand Officers were authorized to set apart or dedicate the Grand Chapter Hall for the purposes of Royal Arch Masonry, and on behalf of the Grand Chapter to invite the Grand Officers of other Grand Chapters to be present and assist in the ceremonies. As this Grand Chapter had been looked upon by our sister Grand Chapters as being excessively exclusive, and as we had never had the pleasure of knowing many of our companions of the Royal Arch of other jurisdictions, invitations were extended on behalf of the Grand Chapter to the first six elective Grand Officers of every Grand Chapter in the world, many of whom promptly responded, accepting the invitation, and expressing their pleasure at being permitted to be present at and witness the first dedication of a room or hall to the exclusive purposes of Royal Arch Masons. Monday the 29th day of September was selected as the time of consecration.

Dedication of Renaissance Hall

The New Masonic Temple was dedicated to Masonry by the Right Worshipful Grand Lodge of Pennsylvania on Friday, September 26th, 1873, and early in the morning of the 29th, the Grand Chapter Officers received the invited guests at the Grand Chapter Room in the old Masonic Hall on Chestnut Street, from whence they were escorted to the New Masonic Temple, which was examined in all its parts from cellar to roof. Early in the afternoon, the companions to the number of six hundred, met in Renaissance or Grand Chapter Hall to assist in the Dedicatory Ceremonies.

At 5 o'clock P.M., the Grand Officers of sister Jurisdictions, together with the Grand Officers, the District Deputy Grand

High Priests, Past Grand High Priests, and the High Priests, Kings and Scribes, of the several Chapters meeting in the New Masonic Temple, met in Corinthian or Grand Lodge Hall.

The Grand Officers of sister Grand Jurisdictions, the Past Grand High Priests and the District Deputy Grand High Priests of this Jurisdiction wore their respective collars, aprons and jewels.

The Grand Officers of Pennsylvania and the High Priests, Kings and Scribes of Chapters meeting in the New Masonic Temple in full official robes and clothing participated.

The Grand Marshal then formed the procession as follows:—

Grand Masters of Ceremonies carrying the Ark of the Covenant, the Grand Marshal, Grand Officers, Past Grand High Priests and the Grand Officers of the following:— The Grand Chapters of Massachusetts, Rhode Island, New York Maryland, New Jersey, South Carolina, Ohio, Iowa, Georgia, Wisconsin, Delaware, District of Columbia and West Virginia. Then followed the Grand Chaplains, District Deputy Grand High Priests of Grand Chapter, the appointed Grand Officers, and the officers of eight subordinate Chapters of Pennsylvania.

The Grand March then commenced and as the Grand Officers entered, all the companions arose with as much silence as possible, and remained standing until after the prayer. The Grand and the appointed Grand Officers having taken their respective stations, and the visiting Grand Officers proceeding to the places assigned them, all remained standing and an anthem was sung, then followed by a prayer by Companion and Rev. John Chambers, Grand Chaplain.

The procession was then formed following in right and left after the Grand High Priest, and proceeded three times around the Hall, during which time another anthem was sung. The Grand Officers taking their proper positions, and taking the elements of Consecration at the proper time, sprinkled the Chapter room with corn, wine and oil. The procession then proceeded three times around the Hall, the same as before,

58

during which two anthems were sung. Then two of the Grand Chaplains read verses from the Holy Bible, after which the Grand High Priest declared the Grand Chapter Room dedicated, in the following words:— "By virtue of the High Powers in me vested, I do now declare this Tabernacle duly consecrated and dedicated to the purposes of Royal Arch Masonry"; followed by the proclamation by the Grand Marshal, prayer by one of the Grand Chaplains, and an address delivered by the Most Excellent Grand High Priest.

The Grand Chapter was then opened in ancient and solemn form.

An address and welcome to the visiting Grand Officers and Companions were made by Companion Andrew Robeno, Jr., acting Grand King.

The Grand Chapter was then closed in peace at 7 o'clock, P.M.

After which a Grand Banquet was had in the midst of beautiful floral decoration, followed with music and speeches. The table was presided over by the Most Excellent Grand High Priest on the right and at his left, the Right Worshipful Grand Master of the Grand Lodge of Pennsylvania. Eight toasts were received in a Masonic manner and fittingly replied to with the final response of Auld Lang Syne.

On May 1st, 1879, the Committee on Work submitted the following report:—

> *"The Committee on Work having had referred to them by the Most Excellent Grand High Priest the question as to the style and title of the subordinate Chapters and the degree of the Royal Arch, would report that at a meeting held April 25, 1879, after a full discussion, decided that the title of a subordinate Chapter be a Chapter of Royal Arch Masons, and that the Degree conferred therein should be called the Degree of a Holy Royal Arch Mason."*

The consideration of the subject was postponed until the next Quarterly Communication, at which time it was moved to adopt the report, when the Most Excellent Grand High Priest decided that he could not entertain the motion, as by the Constitution the Degree is "The Royal Arch Degree"; Companions on their exaltation become "Royal Arch Masons," and subordinate Chapters are Chapters of "Royal Arch Masons"; the word "Holy" not to be used in either case.

The Grand Secretary reported on December 8th, 1881, that he had received among some papers of the Grand Chapter found in the archives of the Grand Lodge, the original Minutes of the Grand Chapter from December 1796 to 1812, making the records of the Grand Chapter complete.

In a letter addressed to the Most Excellent Grand Chapter in August, 1882, the Officers of Jerusalem Chapter No. 3, wrote, that by resolution they had decided to celebrate the one hundred and twenty-fifth anniversary of said Chapter, and at the Stated meeting held January 28th last, the following from the Special Committee was adopted: "That the Grand Chapter of Pennsylvania be asked to sanction this action of Chapter No. 3, in thus celebrating the introduction of Royal Arch Masonry in Pennsylvania, and also in the United States."

On June 7th, 1883, Companion Louis Wagner offered the following, which was unanimously adopted:—

"Whereas, an effort is now being made by many of the Subordinate Masonic Bodies in this jurisdiction to secure the early establishment of a Home for Aged and Indigent Masons, an enterprise, commanding itself to the judgment and charity of all Royal Arch Masons, therefore:—

"Resolved:— That the Grand Holy Royal Arch Chapter of Pennsylvania has heard with great satisfaction of the movement to establish such a Home, and that

it cordially recommends this great charity to the active cooperation and aid of its several subordinate Lodges and Chapters."

The Committee on Charity made a report at the December Quarterly Communication, 1884, as follows:—

"Inasmuch as the several Charity Funds of the R. W. Grand Lodge of Pennsylvania, subordinate Lodges and Royal Arch Chapters of this jurisdiction, are happily provided with ample and increasing means, and when representatives so earnestly and thoroughly perform their work of aiding our poor and needy brethren, companions, their widows and orphans; that your committee has made but a single call upon the generosity of this Grand Chapter, during the past Masonic year."***

"The committee has given the subject some attention and upon revising the reports of the committees of former years, to this Grand Chapter, we do not find any action has been towards creating a Permanent Charity Fund with the usual Rules and Regulations to govern the distribution of its revenue. The few cases requiring aid of this Grand Chapter heretofore was made to and acted upon directly at Stated Quarterly Communications. Your committee, therefore have not at this time any new ideas or propositions to offer, feeling assured that, should it be found necessary in the future, the Grand Chapter, in its wisdom will establish a fund sufficient to meet all demands upon it for the relief of our Companions in distress."

At that time and ever since, the invested funds of Grand Chapter have evidently been considered as belonging to the Permanent Fund.

June 6th, 1889, the Most Excellent Grand High Priest called attention to the severe and disastrous floods at Johnstown and elsewhere in this jurisdiction, and the great loss of life and distress that prevailed there. He stated that he had drawn an order on the Most Excellent Grand Treasurer for two hundred and fifty dollars, and had also issued calls on the several Chapters for aid. On motion, the action of the Most Excellent Grand High Priest was approved, and a further sum of two hundred and fifty dollars appropriated, if in his judgment the same is necessary.

December 8th, 1892, Most Excellent Companion, Thomas R. Patton, Grand Treasurer, offered the following resolution which was unanimously adopted:—

"Resolved:—That in testimony of the sympathy this Grand Chapter feels for the Masonic Home of Pennsylvania, that the Most Excellent Grand High Priest be authorized to draw a warrant on the Grand Treasurer for the sum of five hundred dollars as a donation from the Grand Holy Royal Arch Chapter of Pennsylvania, to the Peramanent Fund of the Masonic Home of Pennsylvania."

The President of the Masonic Home of Pennsylvania, Companion Louis Wagner, returned thanks for the Home for this most liberal donation.

On June 8th, 1893, the Most Excellent Grand High Priest, Companion Edgar A. Tennis, made an order changing the position of the Altar in the Chapter Hall as follows:— "That the position of the Altar with the Holy Bible opened thereon shall be upon the floor immediately in front of the High Priest's station, except while conferring the Royal Arch Degree, when it shall occupy the usual position at the entrance of the Tabernacle."

Companion Edgar A. Tennis, Most Excellent Grand High Priest, on December 6th, 1894, called attention to the fact that the One Hundredth Anniversary of the formation of this Grand Chapter will occur on November 23rd, 1895, whereupon, it was on motion of Companion William J. Kelly:—

> *"Resolved:—That a committee be appointed to consider the advisability of celebrating the said One Hundredth Anniversary, and to report at the Annual Grand Communication on St. John's Day next."*

The Most Excellent Grand High Priest was pleased to appoint the Committee on Finance as said committee.

On December 27th, 1894, the newly elected Grand Officers were installed, at which time Companion Ezra S. Bartlett became the Most Excellent Grand High Priest. At this meeting the Committee on Finance presented the following report which was received, and the resolution as offered was unanimously adopted:—

> *"Resolved: That we deem it eminently fitting and appropriate that the One Hundredth Anniversary of the Opening of this Grand Holy Royal Arch Chapter, be celebrated on the twenty-third day of November, 1895, and that a committee be appointed in conjunction with the elective Grand Officers to prepare a proper programme for the celebration; and that an amount for the required expense attending the same be authorized to be expended by the committee."*

The Most Excellent Grand High Priest appointed a committee provided in the above resolution, consisting of thirteen outstanding Capitular Masons as the "Committee on Centennial Celebration." The committee was organized and divided into sub-committees.

Invitations were issued to the Grand High Priests, and Grand Representatives of each Grand Chapter with which we were in fraternal correspondence; to the Past Grand High Priests and Grand Officers of all adjoining jurisdictions, as well as to the past and present officers of the Grand Lodge, Grand Chapter, Grand Council and Grand Commandery of Pennsylvania. In addition to such official communication personal invitations were sent by the representatives of sister jurisdictions to the Grand High Priests of the respective Grand Chapters represented by them.

Letters of acceptance in due time were being received, also letters of regret from Grand Officers who were unable to attend, all breathing the spirit of fraternity, with congratulations on the auspicious occasion, and best wished for its complete success.

A circular letter was mailed by the reception committee to all companions from whom letters of acceptance were received giving full instructions as to the arrangements made by the committee after their arrival.

On Friday evening preceding the celebration the Most Excellent Grand High Priest held a reception in the apartments of the Right Worshipful Grand Master, Past Grand High Priest, Matthias H. Henderson, who had freely offered the use of any and all portions of the Temple that might be desired for the accommodation of the Centennial Committee. This reception was largely attended, and was the social feature of the celebration. It was thoroughly enjoyed by all who participated, including distinguished Companions of this and sister jurisdictions, Grand Masters, Grand High Priests, Grand Secretaries, High Priests and Grand Representatives were privileged to meet in friendly converse, and make personal acquaintance with those who had before been known only in name. Friends, made such by correspondence, now met face to face and grasped the warm right hand of friendship, generous hospitality was extended, and each vied with the other in amiable rivalry to add to the general pleasure and enjoyment of all.

PLACE OF MEETING OF THE GRAND CHAPTER OF PENNSYLVANIA,
FREE QUAKER MEETING-HOUSE, 1795
S. W. CORNER FIFTH AND ARCH STREETS,
PHILADELPHIA.

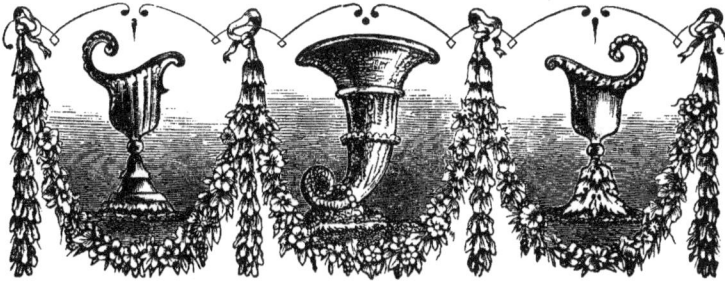

CENTENNIAL ANNIVERSARY

A Special Communication of Grand Chapter was opened in Ample Form on Saturday, November 23rd, 1895, at 2 o'clock, P.M., with an Invocation by the Grand Chaplain.

An elaborate programme was prepared including music, address by the Most Excellent Grand High Priest, and historical addresses which began with the year 1795 to 1895, delivered by four Past Grand High Priests who covered certain years of the life of Grand Chapter. After which Companion Edgar A. Tennis, Past Grand High Priest addressed Grand Chapter on "Royal Arch Masonry and Appended Degrees."

Most Excellent Grand High Priest, Companion Ezra S. Bartlett, then said:— "Companions, the next and last number on the programme is the Closing of Grand Chapter, however, before closing this meeting, I want to call on some of our invited guests." He then called on the General Grand High Priest of the General Grand Chapter of the United States, and the Grand High Priests of Massachusetts, Rhode Island, Ohio, New Jersey and the District of Columbia, the Deputy Grand High Priest of New York, and Past Grand High Priests of Maryland and Delaware; all of whom delivered very brief addresses and thanked the Most Excellent Grand High Priest for the privilege of being invited to attend this outstanding occasion. A prayer was then made by the Grand Chaplain, and the Grand Chapter was closed in peace at five o'clock, P.M. If one will refer to the proceedings of the Grand Chapter for the year 1895, he will be convinced that the committee on arrangements for the celebration of the One Hundredth Anniversary of this Grand Body left nothing undone, and did all in their power to make the occasion a profound success.

To Companion Ezra S. Bartlett, Most Excellent Grand High Priest, credit is largely due for the celebration of the first hundred years of a Grand Chapter of Royal Arch Masons in America. He realized the honor, the dignity, the responsibility of his exalted station and labored diligently and intelligently, ably assisted by the Grand Secretary and a committte fully alive to the importance of the occasion, and who spared no expense to make this celebration worthy of the fair name and fame attained by the oldest Grand Chapter on this continent.

Today he said: The Grand Holy Royal Arch Chapter of Pennsylvania is honored and respected throughout the civilized world, and is in friendly correspondence with all legitimately constituted Grand Chapters. May the success which has crowned the first century of her existence, continue throughout all time, and may the century we are now about entering upon be more glorious than that which closes with this celebration."

The banquet was held at 6:30 P.M., when about one hundred and fifty Grand Officers and invited guests assembled in the Library Hall and proceeded to the Grand Banquet Room which was beautifully decorated. The centre of the tables was banked with continuous pots of ferns, among which was a profusion of roses and chrysanthemums, and interspersed among them were floral designs of the Plumb, Level, Square and Compasses, Mallet and Chisel, Keystone, Grand High Priest's Jewel, and other appropriate emblems. On the table in front of the Grand High Priest was a large floral completed Arch, and around the walls of the room were scattered with numerous palms, and lines of flowers, making a wonderful display of decorative art.

The elaborate menu with all its delicacies provided by the caterer was printed on hand made paper manufactured by the well known Wilcox Paper Mill.

The souvenir, a special design prepared for this outstanding celebration was a silver Cup with a broad ring at the top, engraved with the inscription 1795-G.H.R.A.C.-1895, supported by the spade, pick and crow-bar tied together with the cable-tow, and was presented to all the companions who attended this occasion.

The Most Excellent Grand High Priest then called upon the Right Worshipful Grand Master of the Grand Lodge of Pennsylvania, Brother Matthias H. Henderson, who was a Past Grand High Priest of this Grand Chapter to respond to the toast, "The Right Worshipful Grand Lodge of Free and Accepted Masons of Pennsylvania." Following the splendid address delivered by the Grand Master, the Most Excellent Grand High Priest called upon the Most Excellent General Grand High Priest of the General Grand Chapter of the United States to respond to the second sentiment of the evening.

At the conclusion of the banquet, Companion William J. Kelly having been designated as toastmaster, conducted the closing exercises, with calling upon prominent Grand Officers from other Grand Jurisdictions and Past Grand Officers of various Grand Bodies throughout our own Keystone State.

Knowing it was impossible for all of the members of subordinate Chapters to be present, and participate in this celebration, the Most Excellent Grand High Priest directed the Grand Secretary to send out a form letter requesting that each Chapter celebrate the event in its own Chapter Hall, at either the Stated meeting following the Twenty-Third of November, or if preferred, at a Special meeting as near conveniently may be to that date.

Special services commemorative of the Centennial of the Grand Chapter were held by many of the subordinate Chapters throughout the Jurisdiction, and reports of some of the Chapters were printed in the proceedings of the Grand Chapter for the year 1895.

At the Quarterly Communication held December 5th, 1895, the Committee on "Centennial Anniversary" reported as follows:—

Companions:—

> *"The Anniversary Committee appointed under resolution of Grand Chapter, at the Annual Grand Communication, held December 27th, 1894, in which they were directed to arrange, prepare and carry out a programme to celebrate the One Hundredth Anniversary of this Grand Chapter, creditable to the Grand Chapter, beg leave to report they exercised their best discretion and ability and from the encomiums expressed by the distinguished visitors, the committee believe they succeeded in presenting an entertainment that was satisfactory to all who participated; and they respectfully ask for their discharge from further service."*

On motion, the report was received and the committee discharged. The Most Excellent Grand High Priest was pleased to return thanks to the committee for its efficient and acceptable services.

The Work in Pennsylvania

The following is an abstract from the address of Companion Samuel C. Perkins, Past Grand High Priest, delivered at the One Hundredth Anniversary of Grand Chapter:—

> *"Some years ago it was my pleasure to visit the Grand Chapter of England, at one of its Quarterly Communications. Their work, as it was then presented to*

me, differed somewhat from the work of Pennsylvania; but when I mentioned the differences, they acknowledged that ours was the Ancient Work which had formerly been practiced until an advance, if it may be so called, had been made, and, in the course of time, changes had been introduced; but they admitted that our work, as I was pleased to exemplify it to them in all its details, was the Ancient Work as it had been formerly understood and practiced by the Craft in England. That work has been preserved by the care of this Grand Chapter of Pennsylvania unimproved upon, and without any modern innovations."

In Pennsylvania no monitors or printed books of any nature are permitted, and the Masonic Law in Pennsylvania is:—

"What is not permitted is prohibited."

Grand Lodge Library

At the Annual Grand Communication of Grand Chapter held December 27th, 1899, Companion Michael William Jacobs, Most Excellent Grand High Priest, in his address stated that:—

"The Library of the Grand Lodge of Pennsylvania, located in the Masonic Temple, deserves the attention and the interest of the members of the Craft, and I deem it not inappropriate that I should refer to it in this address."

"The studiously inclined Mason has not completed his Masonic education when he has learned the work, and carefully studied the Ahiman Rezon and the Constitution of the Grand Chapter. He knows little and has deprived himself of a source of great pleasure and profit unless he has studied Masonic history; indeed,

69

without considerable knowledge of it, he can not fully understand either Masonic Work or Masonic Jurisprudence. The field, however, is a large one and few students are able to bring together in private libraries all the books desirable or even necessary for thorough or satisfactory work in it, many of the books on the subject being rare and scarcely obtainable."

"I know of no place where a Pennsylvania student or inquirer can so conveniently or so satisfactorily carry on his work or obtain his desired information as in the Library referred to, and feeling, as I dó, that a study of Masonic history by members of the Craft is certain to widen and deepen their interest both in the Lodge and in the Chapter. I should be very glad if the Grand Chapter could see its way clear to aid in the support of at least that branch of the Library which relates to Capitular Masonry."

Most Excellent Grand High Priest, Companion Edward B. Spencer, in the year 1900, brings to our minds food for thought, when he asks:

"Would the Freemason of a hundred years ago find himself at home in the life of today? Certainly not, in the sights and sounds that would greet him on the public highway. The inventions and discoveries of past decades, the multiplying of material resources, the broadening of general knowledge, the refining of popular taste in Art, and the application of science and philosophy to modern practical life, make this almost an unrecognizable world when compared even with that of our childhood. The externals of Freemasonry have shared in this change, which yet is one of legitimate progress."

"As a single instance compare the plain unadorned structure in which were held the meetings of the

*Craft in this city in 1795, with the magnificent build-
ing in which we are now assembled; a brother or a
Companion of that day would never be able to locate
himself in relation to these external features which are
so indicative of change, but let me participate in the
work of the modern Lodge or Chapter, let him there
behold the ancient forms and listen to the ancient
ritual; let him breathe genial atmosphere of this
sacred retreat wherein Brotherly Love is found, and
he will recognize the stable foundation upon which
this institution stands. The differences wrought by the
flight of years are but conventional, and the funda-
mental doctrine of unchangeableness in Masonry is
in no sense incompatible with the law of progress
which governs and controls all human life."*

It is mentioned in the proceedings of Grand Chapter under
date of December 28th, 1903, the Grand Chapter continues
to donate one-tenth of its income to that most worthy charity,
"The Masonic Home," thus setting an example well worthy
of imitation by all other Masonic Bodies.

At the December Quarterly Communication in the year 1905,
it was on motion, resolved and unanimously adopted "that
the sum of $200.00 be given to the National Relief Fund for
the suffering Jews in Russia."

Grand Chapter at the June Quarterly Communication held in
1906, gave the amount of $500.00, and 92 subordinate Chapters
$4,050.50, for the relief of the sufferers by earthquake and fire
in California. The committee in California appointed to take
charge of all funds for this purpose, handled the distribution
so systematically that in 1908, the committee was able to return
the sum of $1,389.77, which was placed in a fund known as
"The Charity and Emergency Relief Fund of the Grand Holy
Royal Arch Chapter of Pennsylvania."

On December 27th, 1911, at the Annual Grand Communication, it was announced that on September 30th, 1911, by reason

of the breaking of a dam, a large volume of water rushed down the narrow valley and practically destroyed the town of Austin, Pennsylvania. On October 19th, a check for $350.00 was sent to the Secretary of the Lodge in Austin, who was a member of Coudersport Royal Arch Chapter No. 263.

The Most Excellent Grand High Priest, Companion George B. Wells, on December 28th, 1914, at the Annual Grand Communication, mentions the fact that:—

> *"While this Temple in which we meet, widely and justly quoted as the largest, most costly and magnificent building in the world devoted exclusively to Masonic uses, is a splendid monument to the courage, zeal and foresight of Pennsylvania Masons of the preceding generation, so steady and rapid has been the growth of the Fraternity that it is already too small for the needs of the Craft, and even now our Chapters at times find it impossible to get accommodations to which they are entitled. I would earnestly urge that serious consideration be given at an early date to the planning for a home for Capitular Masonry for the needs of a half century to come."*

> *"This may be done by co-operation with the Grand Lodge of Pennsylvania in changes which must sooner or later be made. I would prefer a building of our size and appointments commensurate with the dignity of the Grand Holy Royal Arch Chapter."*

> *"If there are those who regard this as an extravagant ambition, I would remind them that there are now more Royal Arch Masons in this Commonwealth than there were Master Masons when this majestic edifice was first conceived, and what Masons have done Masons can do again."*

Companion Thomas McConnell, Jr., Most Excellent Grand High Priest, on April 9th, 1917, sent out a letter to all the subordinate Chapters directing that hereafter, until further orders: "At the opening of each Stated, Special or Extra meeting of your Chapter, after prayer by the Chaplain, you will have played or sung, as most convenient, one or more stanzas of 'The Star-Spangled Banner,' the companions all standing with heads uncovered."

At the Quarterly Communication June 7th, 1917, all companions present arose, and accompanied by the organ, joined in singing "The Star-Spangled Banner." During the singing of this National Hymn two silk flags were brought in and unfurled over the altar. At the close of the singing, Companion Charles F. Bowers, Most Excellent High Priest of University Chapter No. 256, Philadelphia, in a beautiful tribute to the flag and to the Officers of Grand Chapter, presented the flags to Grand Chapter in behalf of Chapter No. 256.

Most Excellent Grand High Priest, Companion Thomas McConnell, Jr., accepted the flags in a well-chosen address, calling attention to the similarity of the aims and purposes of the United States of America and that of the Masonic Fraternity. This flag he said:—

"Is a handsome addition to the furniture in any Chapter Hall. It contains the colors of Royal Arch Masonry, with the exception of the purple, which is but a combination of the red and blue. It stands for all the principles which those colors teach; it has never stood for an unrighteous cause, or covered a dishonorable act; it is in place wherever an honest man or virtuous woman may be found; it has never known defeat, and we trust in God that it never shall. The absolute and unqualified loyalty of Royal Arch Masonry to that flag and to all that it represents, is always assured."

On December 27th, 1918, at the Annual Grand Communication, the Most Excellent Grand High Priest recommended: "That the necessary steps be taken to make the flag of our country, a necessary part of the furniture of each Chapter, to be displayed in every Chapter Hall at all Communications and Meetings, and to require that no Chapter can be hereafter constituted without provision being made therefor."

At the above Annual Grand Communication, the Most Excellent Grand High Priest addressed Grand Chapter, wherein he stated:—

> "*Just two years ago, December 27th, 1916, almost the entire world embroiled in the greatest and most horrible war in history; our country being then the only great power not involved. About four months later our beloved Republic was compelled to join in the struggle, and with her help victory has been won in the interest of humanity and civilization. Our splendid men and boys responded magnificently to the call of honor and patriotism. Meeting places of our Chapters were closed on certain days by the United States Fuel Administrator, in his efforts to conserve light, heat and power, in order that more fuel might be available to meet the strenuous demand for munitions of war. Later, all public meetings of every character, including Lodges and Chapters, were prohibited for a time by the State and Local Boards of Health of Pennsylvania, owing to the prevalence of a virulent epidemic of influenza. To meet all the conditions and keep within our laws and usages is the task that had to be mastered and I assure you it has been undertaken and met cheerfully, kindly and confidently, and with a view only to the best interest of Capitular Masonry.*"

At the Quarterly Communication held June 5th, 1919, Companion Thomas McConnell, Jr., M. E. Past Grand High Priest, called attention to the fact that in 1920, this Grand Chapter would be One Hundred and Twenty-five years old, and moved that a committee to consist of the Elective Grand Officers and such others as the Most Excellent Grand High Priest might desire, be appointed to arrange for a fitting observance of the anniversary. The motion was unanimously agreed to, and the Most Excellent Grand High Priest, Companion David J. Davis, appointed as a committee, the five elective Grand Officers and the Past Grand High Priests.

On December 4th, 1919, at the Quarterly Communication, the Chairman of the Committee on Finance, M. E. Companion A. G. Criswell Smith, Past Grand High Priest, offered the following resolution:—

"Resolved, That in order that the Grand Chapter may fittingly observe the One Hundred and Twenty-fifth Anniversary of its Constitution, the Most Excellent Grand High Priest be authorized to draw his warrants on the Grand Treasurer for an amount not to exceed $5,000.00 to defray the expense incident to the celebration."

"It was moved by M. E. Companion, Edgar A. Tennis, and seconded by M. E. Companion Thomas McConnell, Jr., to amend the motion by striking out the sum of $5,000.00, and inserting in lieu thereof the sum of $10,000.00. The amendment was accepted, and the resolution, as amended, was unanimously adopted."

On March 4th, 1920, at the Quarterly Communication, the Most Excellent Grand High Priest, Companion David J. Davis, announced that the committee appointed to arrange for the celebration of the One Hundred and Twenty-fifth Anniversary of the organization of this Grand Chapter had decided that the same be held on the afternoon and evening of Monday, November 29th, 1920.

The Most Excellent Grand High Priest reported at the June Quarterly Communication in 1920, that the Committee on the One Hundred and Twenty-fifth Anniversary of this Grand Chapter had held two meetings, and that the preparations for a celebration in keeping with the dignity of Grand Chapter were rapidly being completed.

On September 2nd, 1920, at the Quarterly Communication, the Most Excellent Grand High Priest reported that the committee on the One Hundred and Twenty-fifth Anniversary had held a number of meetings and had made progress in the arrangements for a fitting celebration.

One Hundred and Twenty-fifth Anniversary

The celebration of the One Hundred and Twenty-fifth Anniversary of Grand Chapter was commenced by holding Divine Services in the Arch Street Methodist Church, S. E. corner of Broad and Arch Streets, Philadelphia, on Sunday, November 28th, 1920, at three o'clock, P. M., when a splendid program was rendered.

A Special Communication of the Grand Holy Royal Arch Chapter of Pennsylvania and Masonic Jurisdiction Thereunto Belonging was held on Monday, November 29th, 1920.

The Grand Chapter was honored by Grand Officers and Past Grand Officers from sister Grand Jurisdictions, namely:—The General Grand Chapter of Royal Arch Masons of the United States of America; the Grand Chapters of Canada, Delaware, District of Columbia, Maryland, New Brunswick, New Jersey and New York.

From the Jurisdiction of Pennsylvania, the Grand Officers of the Right Worshipful Grand Lodge of Free and Accepted Masons, the Grand Commandery of Knights Templar, and the Grand Council of Royal and Select Masters.

The Grand Chapter was opened in Ample Form at two o'clock P. M., at which time a very elaborate program was carried out.

The Most Excellent Grand High Priest, Companion David J. Davis, delivered a splendid and stirring address of welcome to the distinguished guests, of which we regret only a portion can be here mentioned:

*"On the Twenty-third day of November, 1795, there was born in the realm of Freemasonry, in the City of Philadelphia, The Grand Chapter of Pennsylvania, which was formed, established, nurtured and sustained in such a manner that today we can be justly proud of our position among the Grand Chapters of the world."****

*"We meet in the name of God, the Creator of all things and in whose hands are the destinies of all Institutions, as well as the nations of the earth."****

*"Of all the assignments that have been made for this celebration, none are more pleasant than mine when I greet you, my beloved Companions, and bid you welcome on this memorable occasion."****

The Most Excellent Grand King, Companion Joseph E. Quinby, then presented the Most Excellent Grand High Priest of New York, Companion Jerome L. Cheney, who said in response to the welcome:—

*"Whatever may be the darkness or uncertainty that surrounds the history of Royal Arch Masonry in the United States, there can be no question but that Pennsylvania was the Cradle of Royal Arch Masonry here; and there is no doubt that the Grand Chapter of Pennsylvania was the first organized Grand Body in control of Royal Arch Masonry in this country, and that therefore all the other Jurisdictions must look to Pennsylvania for light in Royal Arch Masonry."***

The Most Excellent Grand Scribe, Companion John M. Core, then arising said:—"In casting about for some one to write the history of the past twenty-five years, the lot fell upon and drafted into service one of our Most Excellent Past Grand High Priests, Companion A. G. Criswell Smith, whose tastes and talents seemed to signalize him for that particular duty."

77

Companion, A. G. Criswell Smith, then delivered a most enlightening address under the title of "Introduction," wherein he stated: "In order to connect the history of the Grand Holy Royal Arch Chapter for the past twenty-five years with that of the century preceding, I shall briefly review the history of that period as presented in the Annual Proceedings of Grand Chapter for 1895."

Going over the address of Companion A. G. Criswell Smith, your present historian finds that he covered in brief from the year 1791 up to the year 1920.

The Most Excellent Grand Secretary, Companion George B. Wells, then introduced the Most Excellent Grand Treasurer, Companion Thomas McConnell, Jr., who delivered a splendid address, the topic of which was "Royal Arch Masonry."

Companion Edgar Fahs Smith was then called upon by the Most Excellent Grand High Priest, and gave a most enlightening address, where in part he said: "The Holy Royal Arch is the summit and perfection of Ancient Masonry, or in the words of another, 'the root, heart and marrow of all pertaining to the Ancient and Honorable Order of Free Masons'."

The Most Excellent Grand High Priest then called upon the following distinguished visitors, the Grand High Priests of the District of Columbia, Delaware, Maryland, New Jersey, New Brunswick, Canada, the Grand Zerubbabel of Canada and Brother Louis A. Watres, Right Worshipful Past Grand Master of the Right Worshipful Grand Lodge of Free and Accepted Masons of Pennsylvania and Masonic Jurisdiction Thereunto Belonging.

Letters and telegrams were then read from distinguished guests who were unable to be present and who sent in their regrets.

The music, which added so materially to the enjoyment of this celebration, was rendered by a double quartette and orchestra under the direction of Gilbert Raynolds Combs.

The Grand Chapter was closed in Peace at five o'clock and forty-five minutes, P. M. A prayer was then said by Companion Rev. George W. Wellburn, D.D.

The anniversary was also celebrated by the subordinate Chapters throughout the Jurisdiction, copies of the program being on file in the office of the Grand Secretary.

The meeting of Grand Chapter was followed by a dinner to all those who were in attendance at the anniversary, and during which a most interesting program was presented.

After partaking of a splendid banquet, the Most Excellent Grand High Priest presiding in the Banquet Hall, presented the distinguished visitors, after which he was pleased to call on the Right Worshipful Grand Master of Pennsylvania, Companion John S. Sell, who delivered a most delightful address on "Masonry."

A letter of regret was then read by the Most Excellent Grand High Priest from Companion William C. Sproul, Governor of the Commonwealth of Pennsylvania, who was unable to be present. Lieutenant Governor, Companion Edward E. Beidelman, however, was requested to take his place and delivered a splendid address.

The Most Excellent Grand High Priest then called upon other speakers, Companion and Illustrious John Lloyd Thomas, Thirty-third Degree, Active Member of the Supreme Council, Northern Masonic Jurisdiction, and Deputy for the State of New York; the General Grand High Priest of the General Grand Chapter of the United States, Most Excellent Companion Frederick W. Craig. The last speaker called upon was Companion Edgar A. Tennis, a Past Grand High Priest of the Grand Holy Royal Arch Chapter of Pennsylvania, and who had the distinction of being a Past Grand Master of the Right Worshipful Grand Lodge of Free and Accepted Masons of Pennsylvania, who responded to the Toast, "Our Honored Guest," which was an eloquent address.

79

The Most Excellent Grand High Priest then announced that we have come to the end of a superb and memorable celebration, and now, Companions with fervency and devotion to God, country and humankind, let us all unite in the sweet melody of our National anthem, "The Star-Spangled Banner."

The Most Excellent Grand High Priest on December 2nd, 1920, mentioned that on account of the fact that the proposed new Chapter to be located at Latrobe, Pennsylvania, would be located within nine miles of Chapter No. 192, and this said Chapter had refused to recommend the granting of the warrant as required by the constitution, the Grand Officers had therefore unanimously decided to decline to grant the warrant.

At the Annual Grand Communication held December 27th, 1920, the Most Excellent Grand High Priest announced in his address that on January 10th, 1920, in the forenoon, assisted by the Grand Officers and visiting companions, he had constituted St. Clair Royal Arch Chapter No. 305, at Dormont, Pennsylvania, and on the same day he constituted Homestead Royal Arch Chapter No. 306, at Homestead, Pennsylvania.

On September 3rd, 1920, in the forenoon, he constituted Apollo Royal Arch Chapter No. 307, at the Masonic Temple, Philadelphia.

At the Annual Grand Communication, December 27th, the Most Excellent Grand High Priest mentioned that at the end of the year 1920, Royal Arch Masonry grew in strength and character. Approximately 5500 members were admitted during the year. There were 148 Chapters and two Mark Lodges, with a membership of about 49,000 Royal Arch Masons.

Pertaining to the Years
1921 to 1945 inclusive

At the Quarterly Communication held June 2nd, 1921, the following Amendment to Article III, Section 1, of the Constitution was offered by the Grand Secretary:

"Resolved, That Article III, Section 1, be amended by adding specifications as follows: V. Past High Priests of one full year's service in other jurisdictions who have had the Order of High Priesthood conferred upon them and who have become members of lawfully warranted and duly constituted Chapters under the Jurisdiction of this Grand Chapter, who are approved by a majority of the members present at any Quarterly Communication of this Grand Chapter, after having been duly recommended by two members at a previous Quarterly Communication, and due notice having been given to all the members of Grand Chapter."

At the Quarterly Communication held on December 8th, 1921, the above Amendment to Article III, Section 1, of the Constitution was considered and upon motion, was unanimously adopted.

On September 15th, 1921, the Most Excellent Grand High Priest, Companion Joseph E. Quinby, assisted by the Grand Officers and visiting companions, constituted Ivanhoe Royal Arch Chapter No. 308, at Philadelphia.

At the Quarterly Communication held March 2nd, 1922, Companion A. G. Criswell Smith, M. E. Past Grand High Priest, and the Chairman of the Committee on Finance, offered the following resolution, which was unanimously adopted:—

"Resolved, That an appropriation of a sum not to exceed $500.00 be made for the purpose of defraying the expense of compiling the Decisions of this Grand Chapter from 1795 to date."

Companion David J. Davis, M. E. Past Grand High Priest, offered the following resolution, which was unanimously adopted:—

"Resolved, That the Most Excellent Grand High Priest be authorized to appoint a competent companion to

collect and make a copy of all decisions and resolu-
tions affecting the general law of Capitular Masonry
in this Jurisdiction from 1795 to the present time."

At the Annual Grand Communication held December 27th, 1922, the Most Excellent Grand High Priest said that a peti- tion was received in due form at the Quarterly Communication held June 8th, 1922, to grant a warrant for a new Chapter to be located at Barnesboro, Pennsylvania, when, on motion, duly made and carried, the matter was referred to the Grand Officers with power to act. After due consideration by the Grand Officers it was decided that the best interests of Capitular Masonry would not be served by the Constitution of a Chapter where no Lodge existed. The prayer of the petitioners was therefore refused.

The Committee on Finance at the Quarterly Communication held June 7th, 1923, offered the following resolution:—

"Resolved, That the sum of one thousand dollars or
such as much as may be necessary, be appropriated
to the Committee on Charity."

On motion, it was unanimously approved.

At the Quarterly Communication held September 6th, 1923, the Grand Secretary reported that the name of the Grand Holy Royal Arch Chapter of Pennsylvania had been registered at Harrisburg, Pennsylvania, in compliance with the Act of Assembly.

On September 29th, 1923, the Most Excellent Grand High Priest, Companion John M. Core, constituted Thomas B. Ander- son Royal Arch Chapter No. 309, at Latrobe, Pennsylvania. On October 25th, 1923, he constituted Hanover Royal Arch Chap- ter No. 310, at Hanover, Pennsylvania.

Clothing for Capitular Schools

Companion John M. Core, Most Excellent Grand High Priest, at the Annual Grand Communication held December

27th, 1923, announced that the Capitular School at Pittsburgh
called his attention to the fact that they were much handicapped
in their work on account of lack of proper clothing and furniture. After taking up this subject with the Finance Committee
at the June Quarterly Communication, they recommended an
appropriation of two thousand dollars for the purpose of
equipping the three schools. This recommendation was approved by Grand Chapter, and the furniture and clothing were
purchased and delivered to the Schools at Philadelphia, Pittsburgh and Scranton.

At the above Annual Grand Communication, Companion
John M. Core, Most Excellent Grand High Priest, made a
decision, "that the Book of the Law as used by the Chapters
should consist of the Ten Commandments written in Hebrew
characters on a parchment or scroll."

On October 24th, 1924, the Most Excellent Grand High
Priest, Companion John M. Core, constituted William B. Meredith Royal Arch Chapter No. 311, at New Kensington, Pennsylvania. In 1940, this Chapter changed its name to Dennis A.
Reeser Royal Arch Chapter.

Companion George P. Darrow, Most Excellent Grand High
Priest, assisted by the Grand Officers constituted Crafton Royal
Arch Chapter No. 312, at Crafton, Pennsylvania, on April
3rd, 1926.

At the Quarterly Communication held September 2nd, 1926,
the following Amendments to the Constitution were offered:—

*"Resolved, That Article XVI, Section 1, be amended by
striking out in the fourth line the words 'Past Master
either by election or dispensation'; twelfth line, second paragraph, strike out the words, 'giving the date
on which he was Passed to the Chair'; fifteenth line,
second paragraph, strike out the words, 'who must cer-
tify that the petitioner is a Past Master'; twenty-third
line, second paragraph, strike out the words, 'has
Passed the Chair is,' and insert in fourth line, same*

section, after the word 'be,' the words 'Master Masons
for at least six months,' so that section as amended
shall read:—

"Section 1. A petitioner for the Capitular Degrees, or
for membership shall have some visible means of an
honest livelihood, be a Master Mason for at least six
months, in good standing with the Fraternity, a mem-
ber of a Lodge of Master Masons and capable of
performing all the work in the degrees he applies
*for."****

The proposed amendments were laid over in accordance with
Article XXI, Section 1, of the Constitution.

On December 2nd, 1926, the above Amendments to the
Constitution were again read, and on motion were amended by
striking out the words, "A Master Mason for at least six
months" wherever it occurs.

At the request of more than the Constitutional number of
Representatives, the proposed Amendments as amended were
submitted to Grand Chapter for a Representative vote by
Chapters. The Amendments to the Constitution were favorably
voted upon, and the Most Excellent Grand High Priest declared
the Amendments adopted, to become effective at once.

Companion George P. Darrow, Most Excellent Grand High
Priest, at the Annual Grand Communication held December
27th, 1926, mentioned in his address to Grand Chapter regarding Constitutional Amendments:—

"That by Constitutional Amendments almost unani-
mously adopted at the Quarterly Communication held
December 2nd, 1926, was enacted the most important
and far-reaching legislature passed upon by Grand
Chapter in more than a century of time. The net
result of these Amendments is: that henceforth any
affiliated Master Mason, resident in Pennsylvania, and
in good standing in his Lodge, whether it is located in

this, or any other recognized jurisdiction, is eligible to petition for degrees and membership in any Royal Arch Chapter in Pennsylvania."

"It is now possible for a Brother made a Mason in a sister jurisdiction, who afterwards acquires a Pennsylvania residence, to find a Masonic Home in a Pennsylvania Royal Arch Chapter, without severing his relations with his Mother Lodge. It is also possible for the Pennsylvania-made Mason to attain the summit and perfection of Ancient Craft Masonry (the Royal Arch Degree) without let or hindrance."

At the annual Grand Communication held December 27th, 1927, Companion Walton K. Swetland, Most Excellent Grand High Priest, spoke regarding the Passing to the Chair:—

"At the December Quarterly Communication in 1926, Grand Chapter unanimously adopted Amendment to its Constitution eliminating 'Passing to the Chair' as a prerequisite for admission into Chapters. This question has been seriously agitated for many years and opinion varied as to its practical workings. In adopting this Amendment Grand Chapter did nothing whatever to interfere in any way with the degree of Past Master Mason or 'Passing to the Chair.' It simply declared itself an independent Sovereign Body, and ceased to meddle with, or concern itself about, matters over which it never had, or claimed, jurisdiction. This policy has now been in force for one full year and I believe that it has proven itself beyond a doubt, of great benefit to Capitular Masonry in Pennsylvania."

In the month of April, 1927, the lower Mississippi Valley was devastated by a flood, causing death, suffering and loss of property unparalleled in the history of our country. An appeal from the Committee on Relief was broadcast over the land, when Companion Walton K. Swetland, Most Excellent Grand

High Priest, deeming this an emergency and without apparent authority sent one thousand dollars to the Committee, which was later approved by the Committee on Finance.

Companion Walton K. Swetland, Most Excellent Grand High Priest, in his address delivered on December 27th, 1928, at the Annual Grand Communication, said, that on September 6th, 1928, at the request of Companion James W. Myers, District Deputy Grand High Priest, District 17, I decided:—

> *"That any Royal Arch Mason, member in good standing of a subordinate Chapter under any Grand jurisdiction with which the Grand Chapter of Pennsylvania is in fraternal relation, not having in its Capitular System the degree of Most Excellent Master Mason, may, with the approval of the officers and members, be permitted to visit any Chapter in this Jurisdiction. If the Companion desires to visit a Chapter during the conferring of the Degree of Most Excellent Master Mason he may do so and the obligation of that Degree shall be administered to him without fee."*

The Most Excellent Grand High Priest also spoke on "Clandestine Activities" and mentioned that:—

> *"The Legislature of Pennsylvania, in its Session of 1927, enacted a law giving to all Associations, Lodges, Orders, Fraternal Societies, etc., the right to register in the office of the Secretary of the Commonwealth, its name, jewels, mottoes, emblems and insignia, and when so registered any other person wilfully using such emblems should be subject to a penalty and prescribing procedure in such registration.*

> *"The Right Worshipful Grand Lodge, the Grand Chapter and Scottish Rite Bodies of Pennsylvania complied with this law. A suit was brought in the courts of Dauphin County by a clandestine organization calling itself 'The Grand Lodge of Ancient Free*

and Accepted Masons of Pennsylvania' to compel the Secretary of the Commonwealth to register for their use, emblems identical in character with these previously registered by the Grand Lodge, Grand Chapter and Scottish Rite Bodies. In this action the Grand Lodge, Grand Chapter and Scottish Rite Bodies were permitted to intervene and defend.*** After a trial of practically two weeks at Harrisburg, the jury returned a verdict in favor of the defendants. It is sincerely hoped that this litigation will for all time determine the right of these Grand Bodies to the exclusive use of their jewels, emblems, etc., and forever relieve us of the pestiferous interferences of the so-called Cerneau Rites."

Owing to the devastating hurricane and floods, causing widespread disaster, loss of life and property to the East Coast of our sister Jurisdiction of Florida, the Most Excellent Grand High Priest caused to be sent to the Grand Chapter of Florida the sum of five hundred dollars to be used in relief of the suffering and destitute in that Grand Jurisdiction.

On December 27th, 1928, the Most Excellent Grand Secretary announced the appointment of Companion John C. F. Kitselman as Assistant Grand Secretary, and asked Grand Chapter to confirm the same. Upon motion duly made the appointment was unanimously confirmed.

Companion August P. Kunzig, Most Excellent Grand High Priest at the Annual Grand Communication held December 27th, 1929, spoke regarding the collection of dues, and said that on September 16th, 1929, he had directed copies of a letter be sent out to all the Most Excellent High Priests, officers and members of all Chapters under our Jurisdiction. He called attention to the foreword of the report of the Committee on Correspondence, written by Companion John M. Core, M. E. Past Grand High Priest (Proceedings of 1928, page 105), of which is here mentioned a small portion of his letter:—

"We believe a conference of all officers of a Chapter, called by the High Priest, and the list of those liable to suspension carefully gone over would very materially reduce the number of suspensions. Companions, let us make at least as much effort to retain a companion as we do to get his petition. If we do not then the only interest the Chapter has is in the Fee and not in the best interests of a Brother Mason."

On June 1st, 1930, there was published a List of Regular Royal Arch Chapters compiled and published by direction of the Grand Holy Royal Arch of Pennsylvania, by M. E. Grand Secretary, Companion Joseph E. Quinby, with the assistance of Companion John C. F. Kitselman, Assistant Grand Secretary. This book was compiled with the hope that it would aid in preventing the imposition of clandestine Royal Arch Masons upon the courtesies of regular Royal Arch Masons. It contains a list of 7,011 Royal Arch Chapters, with a membership of 978,636, exclusive of England, Queensland, Scotland and West Australia.

At the Quarterly Communication held June 5th, 1930, Companion Joseph E. Quinby, M. E. Grand Secretary, presented to Grand Chapter a book entitled "Masonic Chapter Pennies," with the compliments of Companions Albert M. Hanauer and Edward A. King, both of Pittsburgh. The book contains a complete record of the Albert M. Hanauer collection of Masonic Chapter Pennies. It also contains a list of Royal Arch Chapters of North America, together with a list of defunct Chapters and Mark Lodges. This collection and the book represent the finish of 30 years' work by these two companions. The Most Excellent Grand High Priest accepted the book on behalf of Grand Chapter, when on motion of Companion John M. Core, M. E. Past Grand High Priest, the M. E. Grand Secretary was directed to acknowledge receipt of the book with the appreciation and thanks of Grand Chapter.

On September 3rd, 1931, at the Quarterly Communication, the Committee on Finance in their report offered the following resolution:—

"Resolved, That an appropriation of $1,000.00, or so much thereof as shall be needed, be made for the reception and entertainment of distinguished Royal Arch Masons from Foreign Jurisdictions, who may be in attendance at the Bi-Centenary Celebration of Freemasonry in Pennsylvania in October next, and the Most Excellent Grand High Priest be and is hereby authorized to draw his warrant on the M. E. Grand Treasurer for the above appropriation."

On motion, the resolution was adopted.

A Special Communication of the Grand Holy Royal Arch Chapter of Pennsylvania was held in the afternoon of October 15th, 1931, in commemoration of the Two Hundredth Anniversary of Freemasonry in Pennsylvania.

A large number of distinguished Companions from other Grand Jurisdictions, and the Grand Officers of the Grand Masonic Bodies throughout the State of Pennsylvania honored the Grand Chapter with their presence.

Most Excellent Companion Rt. Hon. Lord Cornwallis, C.B.E., Second Grand Principal; E. Companion Sir P. Colville Smith, C.V.O., Grand Scribe E., and Sir George M. Boughey, Assistant Grand Director of Ceremonies of the Supreme Grand Chapter of Royal Arch Masons of England; the General Grand High Priest of the General Grand Chapter of the United States of America, and a number of Grand Officers from other Grand Bodies throughout the United States.

Most Excellent Grand High Priest, Companion Thomas N. McKee, mentioned in his address delivered on December 28th, 1931, at the Annual Grand Communication that:—

"The outstanding function of the year, and probably the most notable event in the history of Grand Chap-

ter, was the Special Communication of October 15th, called for the purpose of celebrating Two Hundred Years of Freemasonry in Pennsylvania, and bringing to a close a series of functions and meetings inaugurated by the Right Worshipful Grand Lodge. The guest list was large, and included Companions prominent in Capitular Masonry in their own respective Jurisdictions."

At the Annual Grand Communication held on December 27th, 1932, the Most Excellent Grand High Priest also mentioned that:—

"The Grand Officers and five M. E. Past Grand High Priests attended the postponed Twenty-second Annual Convention of The George Washington Masonic National Memorial Association, Incorporated, which was held on May 11th, 1932, in the Auditorium of the Memorial Temple, at Alexandria, Virginia."

"In addition to Representatives of the Grand Bodies of all the States in the Union and the District of Columbia, which form the Association, were guests from the Grand Bodies of China, Cuba, Mexico, Philippine Islands, Porto Rico and Saskatchewan."
"The meeting adjourned in the afternoon to meet the following day to participate in the Dedicatory Exercises."

"On May 12th, 1932, although there was a continuous downpour of rain until late in the afternoon, it was estimated upwards of fifteen thousand members of the Craft, with an escort of five thousand men, comprising Army, Navy, Marine Corps and Coast Guard detachments participated in the scheduled parade over the streets of the City of Alexandria, disbanding at the Memorial Temple erected on Shooter's Hill. President Hoover and Mrs. Hoover, in company with

several members of his Cabinet and their ladies, graced the meeting with their presence. This was one of the greatest gatherings of Freemasons ever assembled, and the occasion an epoch in the history of the Craft."

Companion Charles H. Weaver, Most Excellent Grand High Priest, at the Annual Grand Communication held December 27th, 1934, spoke regarding a change in Masonic Dress, and said:—

"I am firmly convinced that the wearing of Crowns has outlived its usefulness. At the December Quarterly Communication I had introduced an Amendment to the Regulations, doing away with the necessity of Crowns. I would be glad to have your advice as to what you think of it. I am a firm believer in majority rule and the majority opinion should decide the question. The matter will be voted on at the March Quarterly."

The Amendment, however, was postponed until the Quarterly Communication, December 5th, 1935, when again it was taken up and on motion duly made and seconded, the proposed Amendment was withdrawn.

At the Quarterly Communication held on March 7th, 1935, at which time Companion Albert T. Hanby was Most Excellent Grand High Priest, the Committee on Finance offered the following resolution:—

"Resolved, That in view of the present financial condition, and with a desire on the part of Grand Chapter to assist the subordinate Chapters, that Grand Chapter refund to each subordinate Chapter twenty per cent of the amount of dues paid by it to Grand Chapter for the year 1934, and the Grand High Priest be and is

91

hereby authorized to draw his warrants in favor of each subordinate Chapter for the said refund to be paid out of the funds not otherwise appropriated."

On motion, it was adopted.

Companion Albert T. Hanby, Most Excellent Grand High Priest, at the Quarterly Communication held on March 5th, 1936, authorized the Committee on Finance to offer the following resolution:—

"Resolved, That in view of the present financial condition, and with a desire on the part of Grand Chapter to assist the subordinate Chapters, that Grand Chapter refund to each subordinate Chapter and Mark Lodge ten per cent of the amount of dues paid by it to Grand Chapter for the year 1935, and the Most Excellent Grand High Priest be and is hereby authorized to draw his warrants in favor of each subordinate Chapter and Mark Lodge for the said refund to be paid out of the funds not otherwise appropriated."

When on motion the resolution was adopted.

Companion James C. Weir, Most Excellent Grand High Priest, at the Annual Grand Communication held on December 27th, 1937, speaks regarding Representatives:—

"Just a word about Representatives from our Chapters. Grand Chapter pays the expenses of your Representatives to Philadelphia to attend the Quarterly Communication in December each year. Far be it for me to tell a Chapter whom they should elect to represent them. Some Chapters are in the habit of sending the retiring High Priest. I think this is a mistake, because he only makes the one trip to Grand Chapter and thereby does not become acquainted with the working of Grand Chapter. The Representative is 'Your Ambassador' to Grand Chapter, and should be a live-wire and the spark-plug; or in other words, the most popu-

*lar Past High Priest in your Chapter, and take back
to his Chapter a full report of everything that trans-
pires at the Quarterly Communication in December.
Therefore, I do firmly believe that each subordinate
Chapter would be better represented by selecting a
permanent Representative."*

Companion Walter M. Carwithen, Most Excellent Grand
High Priest, at the Quarterly Communication held on March
2nd, 1939, announced that a "Declaration of Principles" of
the Masonic Fraternity has been presented to and adopted by
Grand Lodge at its Quarterly Communication held March 1st,
1939: said "Declaration of Principles" was the result of a conference by the Grand Masters held in Alexandria, Virginia, in
February last, and recommended that Grand Chapter should
adopt a similar "Declaration of Principles," and submitted such,
which was on motion, unanimously adopted . (See Proc. 1939,
pp. 11-12.)

At the Quarterly Communication of Grand Chapter held on
December 5th, 1940, Companion Albert T. Hanby, M. E. Past
Grand High Priest, was elected Most Excellent Grand
Treasurer.

Companion Frank R. Leech, Most Excellent Grand High
Priest, at the Quarterly Communication held on June 5th, 1941,
was pleased to make the following appointment: Companion
John C. F. Kitselman, Most Excellent Grand Secretary, owing
to the death of our faithful M. E. Grand Secretary, Companion
Joseph E. Quinby.

At the Quarterly Communication held on December 4th,
1941, the Most Excellent Grand High Priest said:—

*"Companion Kitselman followed as Grand Secretary
and has been a worthy successor. At all times he has
been of invaluable assistance to me and always with
a smile. With his experience in the Grand Secretary's
office, he has been able to advise with authority the
various Secretaries as to the conduct of their office."*

At the Quarterly Communication held March 5th, 1942, the Most Excellent Grand High Priest, Companion Frank R. Leech announced that for the duration of the war it is permissible for officers of Chapters who are in the armed forces of the United States to appear in their military uniforms.

The Committee on Finance at the Quarterly Communication held on December 3rd, 1942, offered the following resolution:—

"Resolved, That during such a time as the United States of America is engaged in war, no Grand Chapter dues shall be payable by a Constituent Chapter upon any of its members whose dues have been remitted on account of such service by the Constituent Chapter of which he is a member for the twelve months immediately preceding St. John the Evangelist's Day in the year for which the General Return of members is made. The General Return of each Constituent Chapter claiming credit herein shall in addition to the other information specified therein contain a list of the members whose dues have been remitted and the branch of service in which they are engaged."

The resolution on motion, was approved.

During the above Quarterly Communication, the Most Excellent Grand High Priest announced that Companion Edgar A. Tennis, M. E. Past Grand High Priest, on December 8th, 1942, would celebrate the Fiftieth Anniversary of his election as Most Excellent Grand High Priest of this Grand Chapter, and on behalf of Grand Chapter presented him with a remembrance to commemorate the occasion. Companion Tennis responded, expressing his appreciation for this gift, stating it was an entire surprise to him.

Companion Robert J. Arnett, Most Excellent Grand High Priest, at the Quarterly Communication held March 4th, 1943, said:—

"Many appeals are being made for donations to various agencies and societies in war effort. All these we have no doubt are most worthy, and should receive the support of all Royal Arch Masons individually, bearing in mind, however, that Chapter Funds are not to be used for any but purely Masonic purposes. This does not prevent investing in Defense Bonds and we urge the purchase of as many as possible."

On the above Quarterly Communication, the Most Excellent Grand High Priest presented a check for $100.00 to Brother John A. Lathwood, R. W. Grand Master, to be used by the Masonic Military and Naval Service Committee of the Grand Lodge of Pennsylvania.

At the Quarterly Communication, held June 3rd, 1943, Companion Robert J. Arnett, Most Excellent Grand High Priest, was pleased to appoint Companion William J. Paterson, Past High Priest of Temple Royal Arch Chapter No. 248, Philadelphia, to write the history of "The Grand Holy Royal Arch Chapter of Pennsylvania and Masonic Jurisdiction Thereunto Belonging," to be read at the One Hundred and Fiftieth Anniversary in 1945.

On September 3rd, 1943, at the Quarterly Communication, a most beautiful testimonial of the affection and regard for Companion George P. Darrow, M. E. Past Grand High Priest, who passed to the beyond, was presented by the Committee on Finance, in memory of their Chairman.

When on motion, it was resolved:—

"That the Committee on Finance of the Grand Holy Royal Arch Chapter of Pennsylvania, make this record of the death of our late Chairman, Companion George P. Darrow, as a permanent testimonial of the affection and regard with which his memory is cherished by all its members, and be it further

95

*"Resolved, That these resolutions be made a part of
the minutes of the Committee and a copy thereof be
sent to his widow."*

Companion David J. Davis, M. E. Past Grand High Priest,
at the Quarterly Communication on September 7th, 1944, was
appointed Chairman of the One Hundred and Fiftieth Anniversary Committee by the Most Excellent Grand High Priest.

Companion Robert J. Arnett, Most Excellent Grand High
Priest, at the Quarterly Communication on December 7th, 1944,
said in his address:—

*"Freemasonry is rendering splendid service to our
Brethren and Companions in the armed forces, both
at home and abroad, but there remains for us a greater
responsibility when the conflict ends, and that is the
rehabilitation and readjustment of the returning sol-
dier. To me an individual obligation rather than a
fraternal one, as no group action can take the place of
personal contact and interest in the welfare of these
boys as they return to civilian life. We have taught
many of them within our Lodge rooms and Chapter
Halls the virtues of peace, love of neighbor, morality
and religion, and they have every right to expect much
of us. And if we fail the brotherhood and charity of
which we boast will become as sounding brass or a
tinkling symbol."*

*"We must not allow these men to stand alone and no
greater opportunity will ever be afforded as to put
into practice the great principles of Freemasonry than
the days that lie ahead."*

*"May the Grand Architect of the Universe bring victory
speedily to our armies, abolish forever war with all its
atrocities, and then as the waters cover the sea may
the whole earth be covered with Peace and Good Will
among men."*

The Most Excellent Grand High Priest then announced, "that the coming year will bring the celebration of the One Hundred and Fiftieth Anniversary of Grand Chapter. How and where it will be celebrated is a matter for the incoming Most Excellent Grand High Priest. To him I offer my services in any manner that may be helpful, and have today placed the sum of $1500.00 to the credit of the Anniversary Fund out of my own allowance for expense as Grand High Priest."

Capitular Schools of Instruction

The Capitular Schools of Instruction, located in Philadelphia, Pittsburgh and Scranton, have proven most valuable to the Grand Chapter and the Subordinate Chapters throughout the State. Companion Robert D. Cole, Past High Priest of St. John Royal Arch Chapter No. 232, Philadelphia, is the Director of Work and has served in this position since the year 1921, having assisted in this special work for over thirty-four years. He is well skilled in the ritual of Capitular Masonry.

During the year 1945

The Most Excellent Grand High Priest, Companion William R. Burchfield, decided that during the year 1945 the Grand Holy Royal Arch Chapter of Pennsylvania would hold its Quarterly Communications in various sections of the State.

However, a letter was sent out by the M. E. Grand Secretary on January 31st, 1945, addressed to the Members of Grand Chapter, wherein it stated as follows:

"Companions:

> *"This is to advise that by direction of the M. E. Grand High Priest, in deference to the request of the War Mobilization Director, the Quarterly Communication of Grand Chapter, scheduled for Thursday, March 8th, 1945, at the Masonic Temple, Philadelphia, has been called off."*

97

Another letter was sent out under date of May 14th, 1945 from the M. E. Grand Secretary's office addressed to the members of Grand Chapter as follows: Companions:—

"The next Quarterly Communication of the Grand Holy Royal Arch Chapter of Pennsylvania will be held in Masonic Temple, Fifth, Lytton and Tennyson Avenues, Pittsburgh, on Thursday, June 7th, 1945, at 7:00 o'clock, P. M.

"The meeting will be limited as far as possible to the Grand Officers of Grand Chapter and Companions near Pittsburgh, in deference to request of War Mobilization Director to limit unnecessary travel."

The Quarterly Communication of Grand Chapter was held in Pittsburgh on the above date and the meeting was attended by a large number of the Companions.

Under date of July 20th, 1945, a letter was sent out by the M. E. Grand Secretary to the Members of Grand Chapter, stating that the next Quarterly Communication of the Grand Holy Royal Arch Chapter of Pennsylvania will be held in the Masonic Temple, Fourth and Market Streets, Williamsport, on Thursday, September 6th, 1945, at 7:00 o'clock, P. M.

The meeting will be limited as far as possible to the Grand Officers of Grand Chapter and Companions near Williamsport in deference to request of War Mobilization Director to limit unnecessary travel.

This year being the One Hundred and Fiftieth Anniversary of the Grand Holy Royal Arch Chapter of Pennsylvania, and in order to comply with the O. D. T. regulations, the Anniversary Committee decided to hold a part of the Anniversary celebration of Grand Chapter in Williamsport, to which all Royal Arch Masons in that area, together with their wives and ladies, were invited.

At 5:30 P. M. a banquet was held for the Companions and their ladies.

The Quarterly Communication of Grand Chapter was opened at 7:00 o'clock, P. M. for the transaction of official business.

Following the meeting of Grand Chapter, a musicale was rendered, after which there was dancing.

The Quarterly Communication of the Grand Holy Royal Arch Chapter of Pennsylvania was held in the Masonic Temple, Philadelphia, the birthplace of Capitular Masonry in Pennsylvania, on December 6th, 1945, at ten o'clock, A. M.

This being the time set to celebrate the One Hundred and Fiftieth Anniversary of the Grand Holy Royal Arch Chapter of Pennsylvania, an elaborate programme was prepared by the Anniversary Committee.

Royal Arch Masons at Sight

The right to make Royal Arch Masons at Sight is the prerogative of the Most Excellent Grand High Priest and is of ancient origin. This privilege was exercised at various times in the period covered by this history.

Necrology

During the past twenty-five years the Angel of Death has called many of our M. E. Past Grand High Priests from the activities of life to that calm repose that awaits all who have labored faithfully upon this earth. Let us here again remember these departed Companions, for our hearts are filled with sadness when we look about and find they are not here with us.

Companion John M. Core, Most Excellent Grand High Priest, at the Quarterly Communication in June, 1924, announced the death of Companion William B. Meredith, M. E. Past Grand High Priest, on May 17th, 1924. "Loyalty in friendship, wisdom in counsel and safety in leadership characterized the career of our beloved companion."

At the Quarterly Communication in September, 1924, Companion John M. Core announced the death of Companion Hibbert P. John, M. E. Past Grand High Priest, on July 27th, 1924. "Companion John exemplified throughout his many years of Masonic activity the cardinal virtues of the fraternity he loved by faithfully performing every solemn and sacred obligation."

Companion George P. Darrow, Most Excellent Grand High Priest, at the Quarterly Communication in June, 1925, announced the death of Companion Carl A. Sundstrom, M. E. Past Grand High Priest, on March 7th, 1925. "Companion Sundstrom was an ardent student and accomplished ritualist, and set his face firmly against all innovations, enforced the Constitution, Rules, Regulations and Edicts of Grand Chapter with determination inflexible, and guarded the Landmarks as the Ark of the Covenant."

At the Quarterly Communication in March, 1926, Companion George P. Darrow announced the death of Companion A. G. Criswell Smith, M. E. Past Grand High Priest, on January 15th, 1926. "Companion Smith spent a long and honorable service in the various Masonic Bodies. For him Freemasonry had a deeper meaning, and his advice as to the principles and purposes of our Order was ever sound and wholesome."

Companion George P. Darrow, Most Excellent Grand High Priest, at the Quarterly Communication in June, 1926, announced the death of Companion Henry Oscar Kline, M. E. Past Grand High Priest, on March 6th, 1926. "Companion Kline as a Mason had a deep veneration of the ancient usages and landmarks of our Craft, and a high regard for the real value of all Masonic teachings."

Companion August P. Kunzig, Most Excellent Grand High Priest, at the Quarterly Communication held in March, 1929, announced the death of Companion Michael W. Jacobs, M. E. Past Grand High Priest on January 11th, 1929. "Companion Jacobs was of strong determination and a strict follower of the Rules and Regulations laid down by the Constitution of Grand Chapter."

Companion Thomas N. McKee, Most Excellent Grand High Priest, at the Quarterly Communication in June, 1932, announced the death of Companion Walton K. Swetland, M. E. Past Grand High Priest, on April 12th, 1932. "Companion Swetland was mild and loving in disposition, with an excellent skill in expression, and was respected and highly regarded by all who knew him."

Companion Albert T. Hanby, Most Excellent Grand High Priest, at the Quarterly Communication in June, 1936, announced the death of Companion George B. Wells, M. E. Past Grand High Priest, on May 24th, 1936. "Companion Wells was a valued associate who in life observed the teachings and practiced the principles of our fraternity."

Companion James C. Weir, Most Excellent Grand High Priest, at the Quarterly Communication in September, 1937, announced the death of Companion August P. Kunzig, M. E. Past Grand High Priest, on July 4th, 1937. "Companion Kunzig appreciated fellowship with his Companions and his fine personal qualities, his sincerity of purpose, his devotion to duty, as well as his faithfulness and loyalty will long be remembered."

Companion Walter M. Carwithen, Most Excellent Grand High Priest, at the Quarterly Communication in December, 1940, announced the death of Companion Thomas McConnell, Jr., M. E. Grand Treasurer, on October 2nd, 1940. "Companion McConnell was a real man and a sterling character, and knew the joy and comradeship that comes from true companionship and fraternal love."

Companion Frank R. Leech, Most Excellent Grand High Priest, at the Quarterly Communication in June, 1941, announced the death of Companion Joseph E. Quinby, M. E.

Grand Secretary, on April 4th, 1941. "Companion Quinby's life was full of earnest work, largely for others. He leaves a splendid record of services rendered, duties faithfully performed and trusts scrupulously kept, to his family, his church, his fraternity and to the whole community. He left the impression of his faithfulness upon everything he touched."

Companion Robert J. Arnett, Most Excellent Grand High Priest, at the Quarterly Communication in December, 1943, announced the death of Companion George P. Darrow, M. E. Past Grand High Priest, on June 7th, 1943. Companion Core in a portion of his remarks said, "Companion Darrow was Chairman of the Committee on Finance which revised the Constitution of Grand Chapter, and to his wise counsel is due the fact that there has been no criticism of the Constitution since its adoption." Companion Darrow was kind, genial and a lovable Companion and nothing shows the devotion to duty more than his service to Grand Chapter; he was faithful to the end.

At the Quarterly Communication in March, 1944, Companion William R. Burchfield, Acting Most Excellent Grand High Priest, announced the death of Companion Edgar A. Tennis, M. E. Past Grand High Priest, on December 20th, 1943. Companion Hanby said, "At 86 years of age, this extraordinary man was very active, always alert, eloquent, and above all else, intensely loyal to all Masonic landmarks, all Masonic traditions, and attune with spiritual ideals of a true fraternal life in the living thereof."

"Life's battles fought, life's duties done;
Their faults forgot, their worth confessed;
So let them sleep that dreamless sleep,

> *Our sorrow, clustering around their heads,*
> *Be comforted, yet loved who weep,*
> *They live with God, they are not dead."*

In the final closing of this remarkable history, let me say again what has been said:—

"There is no surer index of the future than the past; that the future does not come from before to meet us, but comes streaming up from behind over our heads." If this be true, then the future of this Grand Holy Royal Arch Chapter of Pennsylvania must be of the brightest character.

Standing as we are now, at the end of One Hundred and Fifty years in the life of our Grand Chapter, we recall the first "Declaration of the Principles of Masonry," as recited in the Ahiman Rezon of 1756, wherein it says:—

> *"Certain it is, that when the first man was formed in the image of God, the principles of Masonry as a Divine Gift from Heaven, were stamped upon his heart by the Grand Architect of the Universe. The same principles were afterwards renewed and placed upon everlasting foundations by the wisdom of His Glorious Son, and they are daily cultivated in every soul that delights in order, harmony, brotherly love, morality and religion, through the grace and goodness of his Divine Spirit, thrice blessed three in one eternal God Head."*

Every year aided in the building up of this, the best specimen of the Royal Arch Craft in existence. Step by step, the work of men has advanced, hour by hour have they wrought diligently, and pieces of work more or less perfect have been produced and set in place. The stone that the builders once rejected has been reinspected and set up as one of the chief stones of the corner, and from the mass of unhewn, unwrought stones, unchiseled in the quarries, a splendid Royal Arch Temple has been erected known as "The Most Excellent Grand Holy Royal Arch Chapter of Pennsylvania," which has grown not old, but is like "Majestic Age" surrounded by perpetual youth.

"Let all Freemasons so behave themselves, as to be accepted of God, the Grand Architect of the Universe, and continue to be as they have ever been, the Wonder of the World; and let the cement of the Brotherhood be so well preserved that the whole body may remain as a well-built Arch."

(Pennell's Constitution—1730)

GENERAL HISTORY

Associations with the General Grand Chapter

Companion Charles Gilman, General Grand Secretary of the General Grand Chapter of the United States, in a letter written to Companion Samuel M. Stewart, Grand Secretary of the Grand Chapter of Pennsylvania under date of August 13th, 1838, stated that he had learned of the separation of the Grand Holy Royal Arch Chapter of Pennsylvania from the Grand Lodge of Pennsylvania. These two bodies being now separately organized, he suggested for consideration:—

> *"Whether it would not promote general interests of the Order for the Grand Chapter of Pennsylvania to unite her interests with the General Grand Chapter of the United States, thus combining in one body the general good of all its parts, and thereby strengthen the whole."*

An invitation was extended for a delegation from the Grand Chapter of Pennsylvania to attend the next meeting of their body. This letter was referred to a Committee in November, 1838, but no report appears to have been made, when on motion the Committee was discharged from further consideration of the subject.

Companion Sidney Hayden of Athens and J. B. Musser of Washington in the year 1854 entered into correspondence with the General Grand Secretary, Benjamin B. French, relative to the establishment of Chapters in Pennsylvania under the authority of the General Grand Chapter. Companion French replied that the General Grand Chapter had, in his opinion, no authority to do so. These facts were reported to the General Grand Chapter in 1856, when that body referred the matter to a Committee, which later reported:—

"That your General Grand Chapter can lawfully claim no jurisdiction whatever over Royal Arch Masonry in Pennsylvania, there being a Grand Chapter of Royal Arch Masons in that State which does not recognize this jurisdiction," and:—

"Resolved, That the General Grand Chapter of Royal Arch Masons for the United States of America has no jurisdiction whatever over Royal Arch Masonry in the State of Pennsylvania."

The resolution was agreed to after consideration. There has been no further attempt to organize Royal Arch Chapters in Pennsylvania under any other Grand Chapter working the degrees of Capitular Masonry.

In 1871 an invitation was extended to Grand Chapter to send delegates to the Triennial Convocation of the General Grand Chapter "as a Committee of Conference to arrange terms of union if practicable," which was fraternally declined. Again in 1892, an invitation for union was received and Grand Chapter referred it to a Committee, who in turn thanked the General Grand Chapter for the invitation. The Committee made a report at the next Communication of Grand Chapter, when the following resolution was adopted unanimously:

"Resolved, That we deem it inexpedient to accept the invitation so kindly extended to us."

The Grand Holy Royal Arch Chapter of Pennsylvania has been graciously invited several times to become a member of the General Grand Chapter, but has declined all invitations. However, the spirit of Fraternalism has always been exhibited between these two Grand Bodies, and while each recognizes the other as an Independent Grand Chapter, they are closely associated, mingling together at various Grand Communications.

Appointment of District Deputy Grand High Priests

In order to exalt Royal Arch Masons it was necessary to receive a dispensation to Pass to the Chair, and there were no District Deputy Grand Masters to grant such dispensations and the Grand Master residing in Philadelphia made it difficult for Chapters in other parts of the State. In the year 1817, the Grand Lodge first considered the appointment of District Deputy Grand Masters, and in the following year the Grand Body adopted a resolution requesting the Grand Master to "empower such of the brethren as he may see fit.*** to grant dispensations for Passing Masters to the Chair," and such authority was immediately granted.

Let us at this period delve into the facts pertaining to the appointment of District Deputy Grand High Priests by Grand Chapter. The first mention of District Deputy Grand High Priests for the Grand Chapter of Pennsylvania was noted in a letter written by Companion T. H. Crawford of Chambersburg under date of December 1826, read in Grand Chapter January 10th, 1827, recommending the appointment of District Deputy Grand High Priests.

In the Rules and Regulations of the Grand Holy Royal Arch Chapter of Pennsylvania, adopted December 23rd, 1838, it is stated therein "that the Officers by appointment of the Grand High Priest shall be District Deputy Grand High Priests,*** and shall be appointed by him at his discretion in point of time and number.

At the annual meeting of Grand Chapter held December 27th, 1848, Companion James Simpson, Most Excellent Grand High Priest, appointed for the first time, four District Deputy Grand High Priests to serve for the counties of Allegheny,

Washington, Lancaster, Dauphin, Schuylkill, Berks, Clinton, Lycoming and Bradford.

On December 27th, 1877, it is noted that the Most Excellent Grand High Priest, Most Excellent Grand King and Most Excellent Grand Scribe, were District Deputy Grand High Priests for the Counties of Philadelphia, Chester and Delaware.

In 1878, Companion Charles Roberts of Chester was appointed District Deputy Grand High Priest for Chester, Delaware, except Chapter No. 198 at Phoenixville.

In 1882, the Most Excellent Grand High Priest was District Deputy Grand High Priest for fourteen Chapters and two Mark Lodges, the Most Excellent Grand King for eight Chapters and one Mark Lodge, and the Most Excellent Grand Scribe for six Chapters for the County of Philadelphia.

In 1890, the Most Excellent Grand High Priest acted as District Deputy Grand High Priest for the County of Philadelphia, and continued as such until the year 1911, when the Most Excellent Grand High Priest, Companion A. G. Criswell Smith, divided the Chapters and Mark Lodges of the County of Philadelphia into three districts, naming them, A, B and C in order to avoid changing the numbers of the other Districts, and named a District Deputy Grand High Priest for each District. He also appointed twenty other District Deputy Grand High Priests for the various Counties throughout the State.

Today, the same arrangement applies for the County of Philadelphia, and it is noted that four additional District Deputy Grand High Priests have been appointed since that time.

Printing of Early Proceedings

In the year 1819, the destruction of the Masonic Hall by fire caused great loss to the Masons of Pennsylvania, in the burning of nearly all their records. The minutes of Royal Arch Lodge No. 3, however, were accessible.

At a meeting of the Grand Holy Royal Arch Chapter of Pennsylvania held on August 4th, 1870, the then Most Excellent

Grand High Priest was authorized by resolution to have printed an abstract of the proceedings of the Grand Chapter up to the year 1860, and immediately appointed a committee to carry out the above resolution.

The committee appointed to prepare this matter for publication submitted their report on October 15th, 1870, stating that from the minutes of Royal Arch Lodge No. 3, and the Grand Lodge of Pennsylvania, they were able to present records which proved beyond a question that Chapter No. 3 (now Jerusalem Chapter No. 3), of Philadelphia, is the oldest Royal Arch Chapter in the United States, and that the Grand Holy Royal Arch Chapter of Pennsylvania was the first Grand Chapter organized in this country. This committee also mentioned, "On examining the proceedings of the Grand Chapter they found the years for 1860 and 1863 had been printed, but a very few copies were available, and the next was in 1864, and for the years 1861 and 1862 were never printed." The years 1865, 1866 and 1867 followed in one pamphlet and 1868-1869 in another, since which time the publications have been annual.

Believing there should be a correct and continued history of the Grand Chapter proceedings, they made their report up to and including the year 1864.

This committee arranged the records under the following heads:—

Extracts from the proceedings of:—

The Royal Arch Lodge No. 3, held at Philadelphia, 1767 to 1787.
The Grand Lodge of the Most Ancient and Honorable Fraternity of Free and Accepted Masons of Pennsylvania, 1791 to 1836.
The Grand Holy Royal Arch Chapter of Pennsylvania, 1812 to 1864.

These extracts will prove of deep interest to the members of the Grand Chapter of Pennsylvania, and to Royal Arch Masons wheresoever dispersed.

When the new Constitution of Grand Chapter was adopted on November 2nd, 1863, to go into effect on and after December 27th, 1863, the title of Grand Chapter reads:—"Abstract of Proceedings of The Most Excellent Grand Holy Royal Arch Chapter of Pennsylvania and Masonic Jurisdiction Thereunto Belonging."

The latter portion of the title was annexed as new Chapters were only to be constituted within its own borders, the Grand Chapter to be a Sovereign Grand Body in Pennsylvania. The title "Abstract of Proceedings" was used by Grand Chapter up to the year 1875, inclusive.

In 1876, the title was changed to "Grand Holy Royal Arch Chapter of Pennsylvania and Masonic Jurisdiction Thereunto Belonging."

In 1878, the title reads:—"Proceedings of the Most Excellent Grand Holy Royal Arch Chapter of Pennsylvania and Masonic Jurisdiction Thereunto Belonging," and continued until the year 1895, when another change was made, which reads as follows:—"Proceedings of the Grand Holy Royal Arch Chapter of Pennsylvania and Masonic Jurisdiction Thereunto Belonging," and has continued up to the present time.

Changing the Time of Communications

On November 23rd, 1795, a committee appointed by the Grand Master at a previous meeting held on November 17th, proposed several resolutions which were adopted, the last of which reads:—"That the said Grand Holy Royal Arch Chapter shall hold one Stated Annual Meeting on the day preceding St. John the Evangelist's day in every year, and occasional Grand Chapters when necessity requires."

Rules and Regulations unanimously agreed to and established in Grand Chapter February 24th, 1798, and confirmed in

Grand Lodge March 5th, 1798, were changed to read:—"That a General Grand Chapter of the Holy Royal Arch shall be held half-yearly on the Third Monday in June and December in each year."

On January 4th, 1813, the General Grand Chapter of the Holy Royal Arch, by resolution was authorized to "hold Quarterly meetings on the Third Monday in February, May, August and November in each year."

January 5th, 1824, resolutions read for "The Most Excellent Holy Royal Arch Chapter to hold semi-annual meetings on the Third Monday in May and November in every year." They shall also meet on their own adjournments, and on order of the M. E. Grand High Priest.

New Rules and Regulations were adopted July 16th, 1824, which read as follows:—"The Stated meetings of the Grand Holy Royal Arch Chapter shall be at 6 o'clock from September 25 till March 25, and at 7 o'clock from March 25 till September 25.

Rules and Regulations were again considered December 23rd, 1828, and read:—"The meetings of Grand Chapter shall be held at 6 o'clock in the evening from the 25th September to the 25th March, and at 7 o'clock from the 25th March to the 25th September of every year, and special occasions at such times as the Grand High Priest may direct."

On December 18th, 1856, a resolution was adopted to read:—"That the Annual meeting of the Grand Chapter will take place in the evening at 6 o'clock, instead of immediately after closing of the Grand Lodge on St. John's Day next, and annually thereafter."

A new Constitution was adopted on November 2nd, 1863, to go into effect on and after December 27th, 1863, "changing the Quarterly Communications of Grand Chapter to the Third Monday in February, May, August and November, and a Grand Communication on St. John the Evangelist's Day in every year. It shall also meet on its own adjournments, and on the order of the Grand High Priest." The Communications of the Grand Chapter shall be held at 6 o'clock in the evening on and from the 25th of September to the 25th of March, and at 7 o'clock in the evening, on and from the 25th of March to the 25th of September.

A change of Rules and Regulations went into effect December 28th, 1871, wherein it is mentioned "The Grand Chapter shall hold Quarterly Communications on the first Thursday in February, May, August and November, and a Grand Communication on St. John the Evangelist's Day in every year." The Communications shall commence at 7 o'clock in the evening for the remainder of the year.

On March 8th, 1883, upon revision of the Constitution which was adopted, it read thus:—"The Grand Chapter shall hold Quarterly Communications on the Thursday following the first Wednesday in March, June, September and December, and an Annual Grand Communication on St. John the Evangelist's Day in every year. The Communications shall commence at 7 o'clock in the evening in the months of March, June and September, and at 6 o'clock in the evening in the month of December."

The Constitution of June 24th, 1897, as adopted, reads:— "The Grand Chapter shall hold Quarterly Communications on the Thursday following the first Wednesday in March, June, September and December, and an Annual Grand Communication on St. John the Evangelist's Day in every year." The Communications of the Grand Chapter shall begin at 7 o'clock in the evening, except the Quarterly Communication in December, which shall begin at 3 o'clock in the afternoon.

On December 7th, 1911, new Amendments to the Constitution which were adopted reads:—"That the Grand Chapter shall hold Quarterly Communications on the Thursday following the first Wednesday in March, June, September and December, and an Annual Grand Communication on St. John the Evangelist's Day in every year. It may also meet in Special or Extra Communications by order of the Most Excellent Grand High Priest. The communications of the Grand Chapter shall begin at 7 o'clock in the evening, except the Quarterly Communication in December, which shall begin at 2 o'clock in the afternoon."

The last revision of the Constitution of "The Grand Holy Royal Arch Chapter of Pennsylvania and Masonic Jurisdiction Thereunto Belonging" was adopted on December 6th, 1923, and published in 1924, as such:—"The Grand Chapter shall hold Quarterly Communications on the Thursday following the first Wednesday in March, June, September and December, and an Annual Grand Communication on St. John the Evangelist's Day in every year, provided that when the day shall fall on Sunday it shall be on the following day. It may also meet in Special or Extra Communications by order of the Most Excellent Grand High Priest. The Communications of Grand Chapter shall begin at 7 o'clock in the evening, except the Quarterly Communication in December, which shall begin at 2 o'clock in the afternoon."

At the Quarterly Communication held September 7th, 1939, the following Amendments to the Constitution were offered:—

> *"Resolved, That Article IV, Section 1, be amended by striking out the words "and an Annual Grand Communication on St. John the Evangelist's Day in every year, provided that when that day shall fall on a Sunday it shall be on the following day," so that section as amended shall read:—*

> *"Section 1. Grand Chapter shall hold Quarterly Communications on the Thursday following the first Wednesday in March, June, September and December. It may also meet in Special or Extra Communications by order of the Most Excellent Grand High Priest."*

> *"Resolved, That Article IV, Section 2, be amended by striking out the words 'two o'clock in the afternoon'*

and inserting in lieu thereof the words 'ten o'clock in the morning' so that Section as amended shall read:—

"Section 2. The Communications of Grand Chapter shall begin at seven o'clock in the evening, except the Quarterly Communication in December, which shall begin at ten o'clock in the morning."

The following Amendment to the Regulations was offered:—

"Resolved, That Regulation 47 be amended by striking out the words, 'and Annual Grand' so that the Regulation shall read:—

"Regulation 47. The Most Excellent Grand Secretary shall issue notices to each Chapter of the Quarterly Communications of Grand Chapter."

The proposed Amendments to the Constitutions and Regulations were laid over until the Quarterly Communication in December as required by Article XXI, Sections 1 and 2 of the Constitution.

At the Annual Grand Communication held December 7th, 1939, the proposed Amendments to Article IV, Sections 1 and 2 and Regulation No. 47, of the Constitutions of Grand Chapter, which were offered at the Quarterly Communication held September 7th, 1939, were again read, and having been separately acted upon, were adopted.

Membership in Grand Chapter

After the Independence of Grand Chapter on May 17th, 1824, it is well to note that eighteen Grand High Priests of Grand Chapter served also at one time or another as Grand Master of the Grand Lodge of Pennsylvania, proving that a close relation has always existed between the two Grand Bodies.

In the year 1824, the membership of Grand Chapter was composed of all the members of Grand Lodge for the time being who were Royal Arch Masons, Mark Masters, Most Excellent Masters, Past Master by election, and contributing members of a Chapter.

After 1871, members of Grand Lodge who were Royal Arch Masons and qualified as above, were no longer admitted to Grand Chapter membership.

The present membership of the Grand Chapter of Pennsylvania is composed of:—

> *"The Grand Officers and Most Excellent Past Grand High Priests. The Most Excellent High Priests, Kings and Scribes of Subordinate Chapters. Most Excellent Past High Priests of one full year's service in this Jurisdiction, who are members of Chapters, lawfully warranted and duly constituted by Grand Chapter, and under its Jurisdiction.*
>
> *The members of Grand Chapter at the time of the adoption of this Constitution, who are such by virtue of their being Past Masters by election, and holding membership in a Subordinate Chapter, according to the provisions of the Constitution in force prior to December 27th, 1871.*
>
> *Past High Priests of one full year's service in other Jurisdictions, who were permanent members of the Grand Chapter of said Jurisdiction, and who have had the Order of High Priesthood conferred upon them, and who have become members of lawfully warranted and duly constituted Chapters under the Jurisdiction of this Grand Chapter, who are approved by a majority of the members present at any Quarterly Communication of this Grand Chapter, after having been duly recommended by two members at a previous Quarterly Communication and due notice having been given to all members of Grand Chapter.*
>
> *Every member of Grand Chapter must be a member of a Subordinate Chapter, except Most Excellent Past*

115

Grand High Priests, all of whom shall be members of Grand Chapter for life.

Early Subordinate Chapters

Going over the early editions of the Constitution of Grand Chapter it was noted that the lists of Chapters were mostly incomplete, and it was rather difficult to list them here properly.

It was customary for Chapters before 1824 to take the name and number of the Lodge under whose warrant the Chapter worked, as they had no warrant of their own. After the year 1824, Chapters were warranted and were given their old names and numbers if they so desired to retain them.

When conferring degrees in a Chapter it was necessary to secure the warrant of a Lodge from the Worshipful Master to which the Chapter was attached, and it was to be returned after the work was conferred and the Chapter closed. Regularity also required that the Lodge should authorize the use of its warrants for the purpose.

Here we must not forget those early days and how under many obstacles and many difficulties these brethren, true men and Masons, met together and with a true spirit, organized for the perpetuation, through all time of the principles of Royal Arch Masonry.

The Royal Arch was a part of the Lodge yet not a part of the Symbolic Degrees. It was treated independently, and while conferred at frequent intervals in the Lodge under and with the sanction of the R. W. Grand Lodge, still it was not so absorbed into the regular Lodge work as to make it an integral part of the Lodge system. This condition existed from the commencement of our Grand Lodge until the year 1790-1791, when the ambition of some of our then workers looked toward an Independent Grand Body to work the Royal Arch Degrees. However, the wisdom of our Grand Lodge created the Grand Chapter on November 23rd, 1795.

Chapters under the new Constitution after 1824 commenced with No. 133, while the numbering of Mark Lodges did not run consecutively, as they adopted the name and number of some particular Chapter. The Chapter law of 1795 required the sanction or the approval of Grand Chapter before they could be organized, nevertheless we do find several Chapters were established without formal sanction, yet Grand Chapter did not take any action against this improper procedure.

Here follows chronologically the early list of Chapters:—

Jerusalem Chapter No. 3, Philadelphia, 1758, warranted 1824.

Harmony Chapter No. 52, Philadelphia, 1794, warranted 1824.

No. 45, Pittsburgh, probably sanctioned 1797.

No. 71, Philadelphia, "Lafayette" after 1825, sanctioned 1798.

No. 50, at the White Horse (West Chester), sanctioned 1799.

No. 72, Philadelphia, 1799—no record of sanction but represented in Grand Chapter.

No. 56, Carlisle, declared irregular, 1802, as not sanctioned.

Unity No. 80, United States Arms, Chester County, sanctioned 1802.

No. 11, Newtown, sanctioned 1802.

No. 51, Philadelphia, sanctioned 1811, warranted 1824.

No. 62, Reading, 1815, no record of sanction, but minutes missing for a short period at this time.

Concordia No. 67, Philadelphia, sanctioned 1816.

Rural Amity (Washington), No. 70, Tioga Point (Athens), 1816, warranted 1827.

Philanthropic No. 104, New Holland, 1818, warranted 1825.

Phoenix No. 75, Charlestown Township, Chester County, sanctioned 1819, warranted 1825.

Western Star No. 146, Meadville, 1819.

No. 64, Greensburg, sanctioned 1821.

Columbia No. 91, Philadelphia, sanctioned 1822, warranted 1825.

Ohio No. 113, Pittsburgh, warranted 1825, but claim to hold No. 45, refused 1827.

No. 106, Williamsport about 1810, warranted 1825 with old number.

No. 43, Lancaster, 1809, warranted 1826 with old number.

Perseverance No. 21, Harrisburg, 1803 and 1818, warranted 1827, with old number on payment of dues from May, 1824.

Subordinate Chapters Outside of Pennsylvania

The Subordinate Chapters outside of the State knew very little regarding Grand Lodge or Grand Chapter with the exception of making their annual returns and paying their annual dues. They found it almost impracticable, although anxious and willing to conform to the requirements of the Grand Body, to obtain reliable and authoritative instruction in the work, and many irregularities had crept in from other Jurisdictions. This was no doubt due to the long distance from Philadelphia in those early days.

Searching through papers available leading to early Chapters under the sanction of Lodge Warrants granted by the Grand Lodge of Pennsylvania, very meagre information was found, and most of the lists of these Chapters were noted incomplete. However, there were located lists of the following:—

No. 7, Chestertown, Maryland, 1786, which authorized No. 15, Fell's Point, Maryland, 1787.

Unity No. 18, 17th British Regiment of Foot, 1783.

St. Andrews No. 40, Charleston, South Carolina, 1783.

No. 42, Savannah, Georgia, 1784.

Union of Franco-American Hearts, No. 47, Port Republican, Island of Trinidad, sanctioned 1800.

Les Freres Unis No. 77, Port d'Espagne, Island of Trinidad, sanctioned 1804.

La Concorde No. 88, then at Santiago, Island of Cuba, 1807, rewarranted as La Concorde No. 117, New Orleans, Louisiana, sanctioned 1812.

Le Temple des Vertus, Theologales No. 103, Havana, Cuba, sanctioned 1817. (This was the Lodge of which Joseph Cerneau was Master before he came to the United States.)

La Perseverance No. 118, New Orleans, Louisiana, 1810 (successor to No. 98, which may have also maintained a Chapter at Santiago, Cuba), Bridgeton, N. J., 1815.

On August 26th, 1799, a number of Royal Arch Masons, members of Lodge No. 21, at Winchester, Virginia, which had been warranted in 1768 by Pennsylvania, organized a Chapter which for some years declined to enter the Grand Chapter of Virginia, but in 1820 it was chartered as No. 12, of Virginia.

On April 4th, 1840, a Chapter was warranted at Vandalia, Illinois, as No. 160, but apparently it was never constituted, as is indicated by the fact that a request for refund of the Charter Fee was refused. In 1849 there was an application for a warrant in Texas, but nothing came of it. Sometime later another Chapter at Bridgeton, New Jersey, was contemplated but it was not deemed expedient to issue a warrant.

Capitular Degrees
Mark Lodges

The only degree recognized in Capitular Masonry in Pennsylvania in 1767 and up to 1823 was the Royal Arch. The ceremony of "Past Master" or as it is called "Passing to the Chair," was an exclusive right belonging to the Blue or Craft Lodges, and the authority for conferring of it by dispensation was one of the prerogatives of the Grand Master of the Grand Lodge.

The Mark Degree, although bearing evidence of a greater antiquity than the Royal Arch, was then looked upon and conferred as a side degree, and by many considered as a part of the Fellowcraft Degree.

119

The warranting of separate Mark Lodges and separate Most Excellent Masters' Lodges were authorized by the Constitution of Grand Chapter adopted in 1824. The early records are not complete and show that after 1824, at least twenty-one Mark Lodges were warranted in Pennsylvania. It was not until the year 1824, that these two degrees were officially recognized. However, there is a record of the Mark Degree being conferred in 1795, and of the Most Excellent Masters' Degree in 1796.

This recognition was caused by the progress of Royal Arch Masonry in the other States of the Union, and the fact that the Companions of Pennsylvania not being in possession of the Mark and Most Excellent Masters Degrees were deprived of the pleasure of visiting neighboring Chapters. Strong efforts were made, both in the Grand Lodge and the Grand Chapter to make these degrees a portion of the Royal Arch. After much discussion, and the Grand Lodge having time and time again expressed its opinion that Ancient Masonry consisted of three degrees, including the Royal Arch, a separation was brought about on May 17th, 1824, when the Grand Chapter became independent, and Mark Master and Most Excellent Master were recognized as belonging to Royal Arch Masonry,—the Grand Lodge maintaining its control of the "Passing to the Chair," or Past Master.

By the year 1863 only three Mark Lodges remained, all in Philadelphia, although several Mark Lodges prior to 1824 were organized throughout the State.

Prior to 1868, a Master Mason was eligible to the Mark Degree without having been "Passed to the Chair." From 1868 until 1926, Passing to the Chair was a prerequisite for every petitioner to a Mark Lodge or Chapter.

The records show the following Mark Lodges as chartered after 1824:—

Columbia No. 91, Philadelphia, 1825.
Concordia No. 67, Philadelphia, 1825.
Greensburg, 1825.

120

Schuylkill No. 138, Orwigsburg, 1825.
Good Samaritan No. 139, Gettysburg, 1826.
Standard No. 51, Philadelphia, 1827.
                Germantown, 1827.
                Lebanon, 1827.
                Norristown, 1827.
Friendship No. —, Moorestown, 1827.
Downingtown No. —, Downingtown, 1828.
Golden Rule No. —, Landisburg, 1828.
Kensington No. 211, Kensington, 1828.
Roxborough No. —, Manayunk, 1828.
                Abington, 1828.
Northampton No. 212, Easton, 1837.
Zerubbabel No. 213, Philadelphia, 1839.
Girard No. 214, Philadelphia, 1847.
                Carlisle, 1848.
Unity No. 215, Kittaning, 1851.
Excelsior No. 216, Philadelphia, 1854.

A Mark Lodge, Rural Amity No. 70, at Tioga Point (Athens) was opened on September 11th, 1806, and in 1811, as we have seen, developed into a Chapter. Perseverance Lodge No. 21, in 1818, and Lodge No. 106, about 1810, had Mark Lodges in operation.

A Mark Lodge was conducted from 1808, under the warrant of Union Lodge No. 108, then at Wysox and Orwell, later at Towanda, and although the records are incomplete, the brethren seemed to have conferred the degree without authority, as late as and possibly later than 1841.

In October, 1822, a Mark Lodge was organized in Wilkes-Barre under the warrant of Lodge No. 61; it ceased about 1824.

As early as 1816 and until 1824, a Mark Lodge worked at Pittsburgh under the warrant of Ohio Lodge No. 113.

We have seen that Ohio Lodge No. 113, claimed the priority of No. 45, which, however, was not recognized by Grand Chapter. There was close cooperation between these two Pittsburgh Lodges, and it would seem that while the movement toward the Royal Arch originated in No. 45, as early as 1797, it was No. 113, which later became more active with respect to that degree and to the Mark Degree. It may well be that the Royal Arch was worked in Pittsburgh under the then military warrant of Lodge No. 19, as early as 1767, but definite records are lacking.

There are traces of a Mark Lodge and of a Chapter working in 1821 under the warrant of Washington Lodge No. 164, at Washington, and it is possible that these and other degrees were worked in many sections of the State not only before but also after 1824, even though such working of the Royal Arch, and after 1824, of the Mark Degree, without the sanction of Grand Chapter was irregular. That very irregularity may explain why such actions would not be entered on the Lodge Minutes. The lack of such entries in the minutes which exist and the loss of the Minutes of many Lodges make it impossible to ascertain the complete facts with respect to these degrees. And of course there is no assurance that the Most Excellent Master's Degree, as worked in Chapter No. 3, in 1796, was the degree of that name as we have it today.

As showing the popularity of the Mark Lodges in Philadelphia, the records of Columbia Chapter No. 91, show that from 1825 to 1872, both inclusive, only 59 brethren were marked, while the Most Excellent Degree was conferred on 715, and the Royal Arch on 730. Therefore, at least 656 Mark Master Masons, members of Mark Lodges, petitioned the Chapter for the remaining degrees.

There are only two Mark Lodges remaining at the present time, viz:—Girard Mark Lodge No. 214, chartered in 1847, and Excelsior Mark Lodge No. 216, chartered in 1854, which hold their monthly meetings in the Masonic Temple, Broad and Filbert Streets, Philadelphia.

Most Excellent Masters Degree

The Most Excellent Masters Degree was peculiarly of American origin, but it did not appeal to the many Royal Arch Masons as it seemed not to be popular with the Companions, and they declined to accept it when their Chapters were authorized to confer it after the Independence of the Grand Chapter of Pennsylvania in 1824 by the Royal Arch Chapters subordinate to it.

The title "Most Excellent," however, may have been what was then known as "Super Excellent" and it was only considered as a side degree about 1820. Harmony Chapter, the second Chapter in age, did not confer the "Most Excellent" until 1822, when it required about thirty minutes to confer the degree upon three candidates.

A warrant was granted for a Most Excellent Masters Lodge to be held in Philadelphia on January 10th, 1827, "as soon as the Most Excellent Grand High Priest is satisfied that all the regulations of the Grand Chapter have been complied with." A warrant was granted to hold a Most Excellent Masters Lodge at Landisburg on April 7th, 1828, to be called "Golden Rule." Records available do not show that either of these Lodges were actually organized.

Royal Arch Degree

Long before Grand Chapters were in existence the degree of Royal Arch was considered by learned Masons to be a part of the Master's Degree, but it has long been separated from it. In the early days of the Royal Arch, Masons convened under the warrants of Subordinate Lodges.

In the "Ahiman Rezon" containing a view of the History and Polity of Freemasonry, together with the Rules and Regulations of the Grand Lodge, and of the Grand Holy Royal Arch Chapter of Pennsylvania, compiled for the Grand Lodge Philadelphia, in 1825, it mentions therein:—

"The first Royal Arch Chapter of America, of which we possess a particular account, is that held in Pennsylvania, anterior to the year 1758. This Chapter, working under the warrant of Number 3, was recognized by, and had communion with, a Military Chapter working under a warrant Number 351, granted by the Grand Lodge of England, and its proceedings were subsequently approved by that Honorable Body, as appears from a Communication from its Deputy Grand Master Dermott. Upon like principles the Chapters were established in Pennsylvania."

The Chapter and the Degree in earlier days were often designated as the "Holy Royal Arch." Chapter Number "Three" was described as "The Holy Royal Arch Chapter of Jerusalem." It was decided in the year 1789 that the word "Holy" applied only to the Grand Chapter, and should not be used in connection with the degree or with Subordinate Chapters.

There is no mention made of "The Order of High Priesthood" until after 1824, as the presiding officer of a Chapter was known as First Chief prior to this date. It was known in Philadelphia and conferred in December 12th, 1825. The Order is now conferred upon the newly elected Most Excellent High Priest, upon being installed to that high office. In earlier days the Order was conferred separately, after installation, and at times in the Grand Chapter.

FINIS